Stop Fighting With Yourself and Move Upwards

18 Practical Solutions

*Anger, Anxiety, Grief,
Let no emotion derail your Life*

Dedicated to my family and to all the people in the world who find themselves alone in difficult times.

Stop Fighting With Yourself and Move Upwards

Editing by **Radhika**

Cover design by **Shashika Idushan**

Index

**Chapter 3: Techniques for Improved Overall
Emotional Management**

Introduction

This book is the first in a three-part series that deals with how to build meaning in your life and master emotions. This book deals purely with practical techniques you can use in your everyday life to control any feeling at any moment. Sadness, anger, anxiety, sexual attraction, broken heart, none of these strong emotions will negatively affect your life, once you start employing these techniques. There are 18 practical solutions featured in this book that address various emotional issues that we face in our life.

Before we go further, you should know how I came up with the solutions and my experiences implementing them in my life. This way, you can understand how powerful they are and how some of them can be dangerous, if not employed in the right manner.

Here is a bit of a back story on me, when I was eight years old, I used to meditate, I used to follow politics and discuss philosophy with adults. Yes, I was a bit atypical right from my childhood. Unfortunately, this meant that I had difficulty forming emotional connections with children my age, and to be honest, I found them to be boring.

Not anyone's fault, of course, I just wasn't into the things other children were into, and they weren't into the stuff I liked. My parents also, for the most part, left me alone because they felt that I was independent and did not need as much attention, and this left me with a profound sense of loneliness and of being unwanted. This feeling over many years translated into a problem of being short-tempered, especially when it came to listening to my parents. If asked to do something that I did not want to do, I would throw a fit, get angry, throw objects around, etc. They didn't ask a lot of me, and my test scores were mostly good, so the tantrums were relatively rare.

At the age of 14, however, an incident happened. At this time, I was staunchly agnostic. While I was not an anti-theist, I still did not appreciate being asked to pray. I had stopped believing in prayer and rituals at around the age of 10. I, therefore, felt that engaging in religious activities, even to make my parents happy, was highly disingenuous. Pretend-praying and participating in rituals made me very uncomfortable. On one occasion, my parents asked me to light some lamps at the family temple, as they had a function they had to attend. They lit these lamps every day, and they wanted me to do it on their behalf on this day.

To say I had an overreaction to this, would be a massive understatement. I protested to my parents, told them I don't believe in this stuff, but they insisted I light the lamps anyway, so I agreed grudgingly. Once they left, I went to take a shower before going to the temple. The first thing I did was kick the bathroom door. It was a door that had some termite damage, so it was a bit weak, and it promptly broke. Just so we understand each other, breaking the door was not something I was trying to do. I was trying to vent some anger. Now doubly angry and not looking forward to explaining to my parents about the broken door, I proceeded to further do some venting by kicking a sofa. As luck would have it, the couch also broke.

You would think that after breaking a sofa and a door, my anger would have subsided, but no. I was less angry, but I was still thoroughly frustrated. I was walking past a room with a big heavy door, and I thought this one won't break, ideal for some anger venting. I then proceeded to kick the door. I was right, and the door did not break. Instead, only the lock broke. I know brilliant.

I couldn't leave the door like that with its lock broken, so I decided to fix it. I hammered the latch, which had twisted out of shape, and the latch popped back into place. My jubilation was, however, short-lived as I realized I was locked inside. The lock did not open from inside the room. There was nothing to do but sit in the room and ponder my stupidity.

My parents came back after a few hours. It was worse than the yelling that I was anticipating. They said nothing. They just looked stunned and shocked and then just walked away, or at least that is the way I remember it.

While I was locked in the room and afterward, I did a lot of thinking about my actions and emotions. I decided, ok, I could no longer throw tantrums like that. I was becoming stronger, and tantrums were simply out of the question. I needed to bring my short-temper under control. It is at that point that I created the first of the techniques listed in the book. With the method, which I call Emotion Substitution, I was able to solve my anger problem in a matter of weeks. Keeping anger under control is a life-long struggle for a great many men. After those few weeks, anger was never again an issue for me. These techniques can be particularly useful for teenagers struggling to control their emotions.

In the years that followed, I experienced much emotional turmoil. I formulated many concepts and techniques to help me deal with the emotional upheavals and live a better life. In 2018 after seeing the skyrocketing figures surrounding depression, suicides, and other social problems in many parts of the world, I decided to write this book. I figured that since these techniques and concepts have helped me live a happier, more stable life, perhaps they could do the same for other people around the world.

The concepts and techniques in this book are a result of 2 decades of my own life experiences as well as an analysis of contemporary knowledge from the fields of psychology, neuroscience, anthropology, evolutionary science, and spiritual thought. My personal experiences range from a 7-year struggle with long-term depression between 1998 and 2007 to meeting and befriending people from over 80 countries. I have engaged with people from all walks of life, met people living in extreme poverty, and shared meals with CEOs of large companies. I have even conversed with convicted criminals and spiritual gurus. Apart from these less formal experiences, I also have bachelors in Applied Computing and a Postgraduate Diploma in International Development. I ran a software startup for 3 years before realizing it just wasn't

for me. Subsequently, I have worked, volunteered with various NGOs working in the fields of poverty alleviation, mental health issues, Millennium Development Goals, etc. In late 2016 I started my own NGO that helps people experiencing issues like depression.
This is me in short. If you wish to know more, please come find me on thelogicalist.com. For now, Happy Reading.

Legal Disclaimer

The author is not a medical professional. All techniques provided in this book, are provided as is. These techniques were developed by the author for his own use and are based on in his experiences. The author assumes no legal responsibility for the users' experiences. If you are someone who suffers from serious medical problems please seek the help of a professional.

Chapter 1
Mastery over Emotions

Why is it important to stop fighting with yourself?

Your mind is a battleground between two decision-making centers of your brain. Psychologists call these centers System 1 and System 2, and we call them our Heart and Head. The battle between the 2 parts of our psyche gives rise to many conflicting desires and feelings. Ending the conflict between your Head and Heart will reduce the effect negative emotions have on your personal and professional life. We should not let the conflicted nature of our feelings become a burden on our lives or that of people around us, especially our children, spouses, parents, etc. The goal of this book is to help you protect yourself and your loved ones from the erratic nature of feelings.

The simple truth is what you feel impacts every decision you make. Your emotions influence every negotiation you enter into, your every relationship, both personal and professional. Your feelings affect how much you trust someone or how you interact with people you meet.

Your emotions affect what you buy, what you spend your time and money on, who you vote for, etc. Your emotions influence every aspect of your existence and significantly impact the life of the people around you. Your coworkers, friends, parents, spouse, and especially your children are particularly vulnerable to your emotions.

Before we learn how to control emotions, we have to know what emotions are. Emotions are communications from your heart to your head. *Each emotional reaction is a decision of your unconscious Emotional-self or heart conveyed to your conscious Logical-self or head through neurochemicals.* Emotions are, therefore, a form of chemical communication. In neurological terms, the conscious Logical-self is the rational thinking part of your brain, which is the primarily the prefrontal cortex. The unconscious Emotional-self is comprised of those parts of the human brain over which you have no direct control and are loosely called the Limbic system. *In less scientific terms, emotions are how your heart tells your head what it wants.* In Psychology, unconscious Emotional-self and conscious Logical-self are called System 1 and System 2 decision-making, respectively.

When you talk to someone, you do two things. First, is conveying what you think to the other person. The second is trying to get the other person to agree with you or change their behavior in some way. Emotions work the same way as all human communication. Feelings do two things they convey information, and they try to modify behavior.

For example, when you feel attracted to someone, what does that tell you? It tells you that your Emotional-self has decided based on a complex set of criteria, most of which you are born with, that the person is a good prospective mate. Your unconscious mind even measures the genetic compatibility of possible partners through the sense of smell. Scientists are still struggling to understand the exact mechanism behind this, but studies have shown that the brain is indeed measuring genetic compatibility. The emotion of attraction thus conveys genetic compatibility and modifies your behavior by compelling you to pursue the person romantically.

Now, you might ask if emotions convey such vital information then why control them. Well, because your unconscious Emotional-self takes decisions based on old criteria and our world is an ever-changing one.

Most of the rules that your unconscious uses to create Emotions are old, like hundreds of thousands, if not millions of years old. In essence, *your unconscious Emotional-self is working with a moral framework that worked for cavemen and women ancestors but not so much for today's humans.*

Let me give you an example. "You will realize the real value of money when you have to work hard for it" odds are most people have heard some version of this phrase at least once in their life. I also have been told this idiom once or twice when I was younger. Have you ever thought why that is the case? Why is it that human beings value something more when we have to work hard for it? Why would you value a car more if you paid for it with your own hard-earned money rather than if someone gave it to you as a gift? The answer is evolution.

Psychologists call this tendency of human beings *Effort Justification*. It is an inbuilt feature of the human brain, which is to say, it is genetic. Consider how our evolutionary ancestors lived for the vast majority of the last 250,000 years or more. They were hunter-gatherers, living in harsh weather conditions with little shelter. They shared their living environment with dangerous animals like Saber-toothed tigers and had to struggle simply to survive.

Food was scarce in the winter and with little technology to preserve the food, they were quite literally at nature's mercy. Anyone who could find joy in hard work and guarded like treasure what little he got, survived, and raised healthy babies. People who found hard work to be, you know, hard, they and their children didn't make it. The children of hard-working individuals flourished and carried the gene for Effort Justification to the next generation.

Needless to say, Modern life is significantly different from what life was even 100 years ago, but the emotional complexes that drive our behavior, however, remain the same. Letters preserved on clay tablets exchanged between Assyrian husbands and wives 4000 years ago would fit in just fine as words uttered on a WhatsApp today. In the example of the gifted-car, the vehicle is the same irrespective of whether you paid or not. The car's functions remain unchanged either way, it can take you from point A to point B, and if it is a good one, then it can also be a status symbol. Why then should its value in our mind change based on how much struggle we put in to acquire it? Logically speaking the emotional value of the car for us should be the same either way, but in practice, we see that this isn't the case.

The gifted-car scenario is a relatively benign example of the Effort Justification phenomenon, but not all manifestations are this harmless.

Today unless you are extremely poor, odds are your life in material terms at least is significantly more comfortable than that our ancestors. Even just 100 years ago, the vast majority of the human race lived without access to good food and medicines. The number of deaths from natural disasters has fallen to 1/8th of what it was 100 years ago. So, what happens when your life becomes so easy? Well, all those traits that helped our ancestors survive in harsh environments go from being virtues to vices. If you are someone who was born to middle-class or upper-class parents and never really struggled or work a tedious job, then Effort Justification starts working against you.

Mostly, when life becomes too easy, you end up feeling like your life has no value. Just like in the case of the car, your unconscious says, "you didn't put any effort into getting this so it mustn't have much value." This feeling makes perfect evolutionary sense and is there to drive you to achieve harder and harder objectives. You hear this sentiment regularly from middle and upper-class people.

The feeling is usually expressed as "***Modern life has left people without a sense of meaning***" or something along those lines. While the sentence sounds pretty fancy, in real terms, it gives people no insight into what is happening. What is Meaning in Life, why are people losing it, and how do we stop it? A small part of the answer we have already discussed briefly, namely Effort Justification, but there is a lot more to it than just that. The answers to these questions are discussed in the next book in this series. There we will use contemporary scientific knowledge to critically look into the question of what is meaning and what people can do to build said meaning in their lives.

Now that we know why emotions or the judgment of the unconscious Emotional-self can cause problems, the question is, how do we mitigate these issues? You need to do two things to achieve greater control over unhealthy emotions. First, give your Emotional-self what it needs to be content. Second, train the feeling generating mechanisms of your unconscious to be more rational.

What does your Emotional-self need to be content? No, it is not what you think. It is not tasty food, lots of sex, entertainment, or anything along those lines.

Your Emotional-self needs a reason to live, to get up in the morning, and face the harsh realities of the world with a smile. To put it simply, what you need to be happy is to find meaning in your daily struggles, to find meaning in your life. The questions regarding Meaning in Life, namely what is it, how to achieve it, etc. are covered in the next book in this series. The next book will be published 2-3 months after this book.

Second, you need to train the emotion generating mechanisms of your unconscious to be more rational, but how? *You make yourself capable of controlling emotions the same way you train to run faster or lift heavier weights and that is through practice.* When we want to run a marathon, we go running. When we want to score high marks in an exam, we study and practice. However, do we train when we want to achieve greater control over unhealthy emotions like anger, anxiety, jealousy, frustration, etc.? No, we don't, we cross our fingers and hope for the best. Even though emotional stability is critical to life success, we train ourselves to be better at almost everything except emotions. Does that seem rational to you? Of course not, and it does not seem logical to me either.

Much like in the case of lifting weights or running a marathon, there is a right way to do it and a wrong way.

Practice the techniques listed in this book and you can increase your control over your emotions. You need to start small and then work your way upwards. Doing it the right way will bring you massive benefits in terms of life satisfaction.

We will start by looking at the technique of Emotion Substitution.

Base Technique 1: Emotion Substitution (Bring any Emotion under control in an instant)

Have you ever been told by someone to just think about something else when you are feeling anxious, sad, or angry? Have you then thought to yourself, "If I could just think of something else and get rid of my emotions, don't you think I would have"? Well, you are not alone, when I was depressed, I got this suggestion regularly. People would say, just get over it, focus on other things, to say I found this advice annoying would be an understatement.

See, the thing is, people are not entirely wrong, thinking something else can work. Only, they mix up a couple of essential details on how to do it.
Distracting yourself, or focusing on something else does work, but only if that something can produce a sufficiently strong emotional response.

For example, if you are someone with short-temper and you try to count down from 10 to calm yourself when angry, it is not likely to work. If you, on the other hand, think about your favorite movie or football match or someone you love whenever you get agitated, then that would calm you down.

The difference here is, counting down from 10 does not produce any feeling, but thinking about something that makes you happy will trigger a countering emotion. Here you are not just distracting yourself, you are countering one emotion with another or Emotion Substitution. In our example, we countered anger with happiness, so anger is the starting-emotion, happiness is the counter-emotion, and your favorite film is the trigger-thought for the counter-emotion. When substituting, the intensity of the emotions is an essential factor to keep in mind.

If the trigger-thought you are using to produce the counter-emotion is not strong enough, then it won't be as effective. For example, the feeling you get from thinking about your favorite movie will be less impactful than what you get from thinking about someone you love. Your favorite film will, therefore, be a less effective counter-emotion generator than say the memory of your child taking his first step.

Your counter-emotion should be equally intense or even more intense than the starting-emotion.

Emotion substitution is similar to mixing hot water and cold water to create optimum temperature. Emotions are a result of neurochemicals released into the bloodstream by the brain. If you trigger two opposing emotions of the same intensity, the neurochemicals will kind of cancel each other out. The emotional processes are more complicated than I am making them out to be. Still, the water-mixing analogy is a simple way to conceptualize what is happening in the brain.

Another practical easy to use counter-emotion is disgust. For example, picturing something disgusting in your mind, like putrefying food or something else you are disgusted by, will deflect any other emotion.

Consider this scenario, a particularly delicious cake is tempting you, but the problem is you have diabetes. You can't eat cake, it's dangerous, and you could end up in the hospital. What do you do? Do you bite down, tell your unconscious Emotional-self that its desires don't matter, and try to walk away?

Telling your Emotional-self that its desires and judgments don't matter is what we call suppressing of emotions. You should know suppressing emotions is a bad idea. Every time you tell your unconscious Emotional-self that its desires don't matter, it will get a little more upset. A day will come when your Emotional-self will refuse to surrender. It will say, "No, today you are not walking away, today you are eating cake," and then you are stuck.

Also, telling your Emotional-self that you don't care about it wants, will make it care less about what you want as well. *Like all human relationships, the bond between your head and heart is also a two-way street, you get what you give.*

So how do you walk away from the cake without upsetting your Emotional-self? Well, have you ever tried to distract a child with something so that you could feed it?

Your Emotional-self is your inner-child, and you can divert it with Emotion substitution. While you can use many emotions to distract your inner-child, if your goal is not to eat cake, then the best feeling to use is disgust.

When your inner-child asks you to eat cake, picture something in your mind that you find disgusting like putrefying food teeming with maggots. The feeling of disgust your Emotional-self experiences from that mental image of maggot-infested food will quickly cure it of any desire to eat cake. You could also picture yourself lying in a hospital bed, attached to a dialysis machine, suffering from kidney failure. The mental image that you use depends on what works for you. The picture can be of a bed-ridden you, putrid food, or something entirely different.

Thinking or remembering something that triggers a strong counter emotion in you will override any feeling you are experiencing, and this is the Emotion Substitution way of controlling any emotion instantaneously.

Just to give you some further background, in the introduction, I had mentioned that the first technique I created was at the age of 14. I created the method to control the short-temper problem that I had at the time. The means that I came up with was pretty simple. At the time, I was in a romantic relationship. Due to the loneliness, I felt growing up, and since this relationship was my "first love," I had strong feelings for the person. I figured that every time I got angry, I would just think of her.

My calculation was since my feelings for her were intense, that feeling would cancel out the anger. It worked like a charm. Every time I got agitated, I thought of the girl I was in a relationship with, and the negative feelings subsided. Just like that, the short-temper was gone. It was eliminated in a matter of weeks, and I thought wow great this works. The problem was, unbeknownst to me, I had done something I had not intended to do. Unwittingly, I had used classical conditioning to suppress one of the basic human emotions, namely anger, permanently.

Because I had used this technique every time I got agitated, I had accidentally trained my mind to think of her whenever I got angry. Just like you teach yourself to ride a bike by practicing riding, I had taught my unconscious mind how to deal with the emotion of anger. Once this process became automatic, two things happened.
One, I only got angry once in the next seven years, until I reintegrated anger into my personality. Two, my emotional dependence on my relationship increased, which is to say, my emotions for my then-girlfriend intensified. The only time I got angry in those seven years was when I first went into depression, and that was the result of getting overwhelmed by a lot of negative feelings than anger.

I was emotionally vulnerable before this because of my childhood loneliness. Still, the technique subverted anger to the point where I no longer felt a desire to stand up for myself. Rage is a critical part of the flight or fight instinct. When someone hurts us emotionally or physically, we get angry, and that helps us stand up for ourselves. Like most teenage relationships, my relationship was tumultuous, with many breakups and fights. The problem was whenever there was a fight, instead of feeling anger or some desire to stand up for myself, I only felt affection.

As a consequence, after my first break up, I went into a deep depression. I was suicidal. I self-harmed. For the next seven years, even after the emotional significance of my relationship had passed, I was depressed. I came out of depression only after I found a way to reintegrate anger into my personality.

Now, it is certainly possible that I would have gone into depression even if I had never used the emotion substitution technique. However, I am reasonably sure I would not have stayed depressed for seven long years if it was not for my lack of anger. Why am I telling you this? I want you to understand the capabilities of the techniques I am going to share with you.

Since my initial mishap, I have created many more techniques and used them successfully on myself, and for the past decade, I have lived a great life. As of the time I am writing this article, it has been 12 years since I dragged myself out of depression, using a technique I created. Though that method, I will not be sharing here because, honestly, it is too dangerous to use if you don't know what you are doing. The following is a critical advisory for when using the techniques,

Do not use any of these techniques, or any alteration of them that you might come up with yourself, to override any emotion EVERY SINGLE TIME. Allow the feeling to function naturally every so often so that it doesn't get suppressed.

If you subvert an emotion using any of these techniques every time you experience it, your unconscious will get conditioned to deal with that specific emotion in that manner. If a feeling gets permanently subverted, then that can have unforeseeable consequences. Ultimately all emotions are necessary, and if they weren't, you wouldn't be experiencing them. Each of the feelings exists because they helped our evolutionary ancestors to survive, reproduce, and thrive, so do not suppress any emotion on purpose.

It is the excesses of emotions that should be controlled, not the feeling itself.

One way to avoid the Classical Conditioning problem is to use multiple techniques to deal with an emotion. That way, your unconscious will not get conditioned. That said, I repeat, **DO NOT SUPPRESS ANY EMOTION EVERY SINGLE TIME YOU EXPERIENCE IT**. Now, feelings do malfunction, and in many ways, human emotional systems are out of date with the needs of the modern world. However, our understanding of how different emotions influence each other is not good enough for us to determine which feelings are essential, and which should be discarded. Each technique will contain guidance on how they should not be used, so please take note of those.

There are three usage advisories with this technique. I have written the first two in capital letters to highlight just how important they are. Emotion *Substitution is used in multiple other emotion-control methods I will be covering in other articles, so these advisories are doubly important.*

1. USE DIFFERENT MEMORIES TO DEFLECT SAME EMOTION AT DIFFERENT TIMES.

Do not use the same trigger-thought or memory all the time to counter one emotion. If you do so, classical conditioning will take place. What does that mean? Every time that particular feeling arises in you, the trigger-thought will also be remembered, this is what happened with me 20 years ago. If one emotion and trigger-memory get coupled, then that feeling will be permanently deflected. To access that emotion again, you will have to decouple the trigger-thought from it, which is not easy. You can use the one trigger-thought intermittently but not continuously. Rotate between 5 or 6 different trigger-thoughts for one emotion to prevent conditioning.

For example, if one of the memories is a disturbing scene from a horror movie, then another can be a positive memory and so on. When choosing a positive thought, choose something that cannot be taken away from you. For example, you can recollect something awesome your parents did for you when you were a child, provided your relationship with your parents is positive.

2. *DO NOT USE A MEMORY OR THOUGHT LINKED TO A PERSON or OBJECT REPEATEDLY.*

If you think of a person or object repeatedly, the emotional relevance of that person or object in your life will increase. Depending on the nature of your relationship with the person or object, the increase in importance can have long-term negative results. If you use a negative trigger-memory linked to a person, then it will increase your negative feelings towards that person. If you use a positive trigger-memory, then positive feelings towards that person will increase. If the nature of your relationship with the person changes later on, then the strengthened emotions can become a problem. For example, your romantic partner breaks up with you, and if you are too attached, then you could end-up in depression. Another example, if you are put in the same team at your workplace with someone you hate, then that could become a hindrance to your career.

3. *As much as possible, try to use memories that trigger positive emotions, not negative ones.*

This advisory doesn't really need a description, does it? Simply put, it is better to feel happy than disgusted, scared, or angry.

Medical research has shown that experiencing too many negative emotions is harmful to your long-term emotional and physical health. Therefore, while it is ok to use negative trigger-thoughts when necessary, you should mostly try to stick to positive trigger-thoughts. An example of when negative trigger-thoughts are unavoidable is when trying to get over a relationship breakup.

Base Technique 2: Self-Awareness Technique (How to know what you truly feel)

This technique will allow you to find out how you truly feel at any given time about a particular topic, person, or object. Every emotion has a physical reaction that is triggered as a result of it, these are called psychosomatic responses. The tightening of the chest when you are sad, the butterflies in your stomach when you are in love, the feeling of lightness when you are happy, those are psychosomatic responses. People usually only become aware of these physical sensations when they experience a strong emotion because the reactions attached to strong emotions tend to be stronger as well. However, every emotion has an attached physical response, even if you are not aware of it.

Psychosomatic responses, therefore, provide us with a great way of determining how our emotional-self really feels about something. The technique will be described in a step by step manner, but over time, as you perform this method, you will not need to follow each step every time. The key is to determine what the psychosomatic response you are feeling at that moment. Whether an individual will need to perform each action every time depends entirely on the sensitivity of that individual. The method is as follows.

Step 1: Take a deep breath.

Step 2: Feel each breath moving down your throat into your chest, filling your lungs.

Step 3: Similarly follow each exhale.

Step 4: Ask yourself a question about how you are feeling. It must be a yes or no question. For example, "Do you like this person," "Are you angry," "Are you sad," "Are you sad because XYZ thing happened," etc.

Step 5: If you feel lightness in your chest, then the answer is yes. If you feel your chest tightening, then the answer is no.

Using these 5 simple steps, you can figure out how you truly feel at any moment, about any topic, person, or object. Keep in mind, awareness of a feeling doesn't mean you have to act out that feeling. Feeling something simply means that according to your unconscious Emotional-self, a particular event, person or object was worthy of that emotional response. Emotion is simply the unconscious conveying evolutionary logic to you in the form of a chemical release in your brain. Whether that particular assessment of your unconscious or System 1 is a valid judgment is something you should use your conscious thinking faculties or System 2 to determine. Indulging every emotional reaction will simply lead your life down wrong directions, and will make your life more chaotic and stressful.

Being aware of what you feel is the first step in dealing with those feelings logically, effectively, and not letting them overwhelm your rational decision-making processes. Next, we will look at specific techniques designed for dealing with powerful emotions we regularly face in our lives.

Base Technique 3 & 4: Classical Conditioning and Operant Conditions

Classical conditioning and Operant Conditioning are two of the main ways in which our unconscious Emotional-self learns and prioritizes new information. Both of these techniques are central to how the human brain learns information. These techniques are being employed by your unconscious 24/7 when processing data and sensory stimuli. The methods featured in this book to deal with anxiety, unwanted sexual attraction, getting over relationships, etc. do make use of classical and operant conditioning.

Both conditioning methods have been used to train both animals and humans. Carrier pigeons, Attack dogs, Racehorses are all excellent examples of animals trained to respond in specific ways to specific stimuli. People are also subjected to conditioning techniques. A lot of the times, these techniques are used on people without their knowledge. The unethical activity of conditioning people unwittingly is something we will cover in more detail later on. First, we will look at the two conditioning techniques.

What is classical conditioning? *It is a process by which you associate a powerful stimulus like the scent of a food item, to another unrelated stimulus like the ringing of bells.*

This is done to get the brain to respond to the bell stimulus in the same way as it would to food, namely salivating. Ivan Pavlov did experiments with dogs which established the basic principles of this method in the late 19th century.

Pavlov's goal was to get the dogs to start salivating at the sound of the metronome. Dog food was chosen because the response to the dog food, namely dog salivating, was unrelated to the experiment itself. Pavlov used the sound of a metronome as the neutral stimulus or stimulus that elicited no response from the dogs.

Pavlov first triggered the metronome sound and then gave the dogs food and repeated this procedure several times. Afterward, he noted that the dog started salivating upon hearing the metronome. Even without food being offered dog salivated on hearing the sound because Classical Conditioning had occurred. Why is what Pavlov did relevant to you, you might ask? The answer is much of the human brain is very similar to that of animals. In fact, only the neocortex is the genuinely human part of the brain. The neocortex is where logic and critical thinking reside.

Apart from the cortex, there are two other parts of the brain. They are the Amygdala, colloquially called the Reptile brain, and the Limbic system also called the Mammalian brain. The Reptile brain and the Mammalian brain are called so because these parts of the human mind can also be found in reptiles and mammals, respectively. Since there is a significant overlap between human and animal brains, the autonomous responses function in just about the same way in humans and other mammals like dogs. The conditioning techniques Pavlov tested in dogs, therefore, also work in humans. The term Limbic system will be used throughout this book to denote the part of the brain which regulates emotions. Modern medical science, however, no longer considers the limbic system to be separate and isolated from other parts of the brain. It is only seen as one of the many parts of the brain responsible for controlling the autonomic processes.

What is Operant conditioning? Operant conditioning is something almost all human beings would recognize. Whether it is a bonus being given to an employee for excellent performance, or a child being disciplined for misbehaving, that is operant conditioning. People use operant conditioning techniques regularly to train employees, children, even partners.

It is the process by which behavior is modified through reinforcement or punishment. Reinforcements are consequences (like a salary bonus) that increase the chances of an action being repeated. Conversely, Punishments decrease the chances of a particular behavior happening again.

Using operant conditioning will result in the brain associating a particular behavior with a positive or negative outcome. Operant conditioning technique where someone is rewarded is called reinforcement. When a negative consequence is meted out, then it is called punishment.

Reinforcement itself can be positive or negative. An example of Positive Reinforcement would be a child being bought a bicycle for scoring high in an exam. Negative reinforcement would be the removal of an offensive stimulus from the environment. For example, an unpleasant noise being turned off at the press of a button. Punishments also come in two varieties positive and negative. Positive Punishments are adverse outcomes to dissuade someone from acting a certain way, such as pain from being struck. Negative Punishments is withholding of a positive consequence.

An example of negative punishment would be a child not being allowed to watch his favorite cartoon if he didn't complete his homework. If Reinforcements or Punishments are stopped, then the behavior-modifying conditioning ceases. Afterward, the probability of behavior happening or not happening reduces each time the practice is engaged in without the application of positive or negative consequence. Eventually, the likelihood of the conduct occurring goes back to what it was before the use of operant conditioning, this is called Extinguishing.

The potency of the conditioning increases with the intensity of the consequence. In other words, the bigger the bonus given, more interested an employee will be in making sure he is productive. Another factor that affects the strength of conditioning is how soon after completion of a task, the reinforcement or punishment is applied. Punishments meted out right after someone doing something wrong will be more effective in preventing future bad behavior, than punishment a day later. The third factor that affects conditioning is how regularly consequences are applied. If particular conduct is only reinforced or punished occasionally, then the conditioning will take longer. However, conditioning achieved through the intermittent application of consequence will take longer to undo.

The terms are not significant for our purposes. They have been included here, just for the sake of completeness. However, it is always useful to understand the underlying principles involved when we are using any technique or tool.

There are two things to be noted here, *one Operant Conditioning is benign, and its effects, whether positive or negative, fade with time. Two, Classical Conditioning can have unintended side effects and is best avoided except in very specific contexts.* Special advisories are given with those techniques, where care must be taken.

Base Technique 5: Creating Emotionally Potent Personalized Affirmations

What is an affirmation? Affirmation is any word, phrase, or sentence that provides emotional support or encouragement. For example, "Yes, you can do it" can be an affirmative sentence, if it is said to give someone confidence. You should repeat affirmations to yourself, is advice that is often given to people who suffer from depression, anxiety, etc. Most people, however, find that affirmations don't work for them. Why do affirmative phrases work for some people and don't work for some others? The reason here again is Emotions. Affirmations work when they are capable of triggering a strong emotion.

An affirmative phrase that is emotionally potent for one person might have no emotional resonance for someone else. For instance, repeating the phrase "I can do it" over and over again will not relieve stage fright, not unless the words mean something to you emotionally. The mechanism by which affirmations usually work is a combination of classical conditioning and emotion substitution. Therefore the same rules apply here as well. The success of an affirmation phrase at relieving a particular emotional problem depends entirely on the strength of the emotion that the affirmation triggers.

How then can you create an affirmation that works for you? **The key is to combine a phrase or word with an emotionally potent memory or an emotional state using Classical Conditioning.**

Effective affirmations are created when a memory or emotion becomes attached to a phrase during memory formation. Classical Conditioning (CC) is used as an indexing technique by the brain for recalling memories. An example would be you remembering a romantic date with someone when you smell the perfume the person was wearing that day. A memory getting retrieved when you detect a familiar scent is an example of CC at work.

Classical Conditioning occurs as a result of how the human brain records and stores memories. All sensory input recorded at the time of memory formation is indexed and cross-referenced as a part of it.

An everyday example of indexing is a page number and index in a book. Page numbers have nothing to do with the contents of a book but help you locate specific text. Similarly, a familiar scent may have nothing to do with the main subject of memory but still serves as an index for its retrieval. You can use this feature of the human brain to turn a phrase into an index for a particular emotionally potent memory.
Following is the step by step guide to creating an affirmation using Classical Conditioning.

Step 1: *Pick a word or a phrase to turn into an affirmation.*
For instance, names of deities like Jesus, Krishna, Allah or phrases like Hare Rama Hare Krishna, Allahu Akbar, Praise Jesus, etc. work as affirmations and trigger positive emotions. For people with faith, these words have substantial emotional weight. Repeating these words then triggers associated memories and emotions, making religious or faithful individuals feel happy.

Any phrase or word can be turned into an affirmative one. I, however, would advise you not to choose names of people you care about, and this is because the relationships can sour at a later date.

Also, using a person's name as an affirmative phrase will increase the intensity of your feelings for the person, and that is best avoided. If you are creating an affirmation, it is preferable to pick a phrase or word, which has a similar meaning to what you are trying to accomplish. Try to choose a phrase that is emotionally neutral so that attaching new emotions or memories to the words can be done without issue. For example, if you are trying to shore up your confidence phrases like "I can do it," "I am awesome," etc. would do the trick.

Step 2: *Start by repeating your chosen Affirmation phrase over and over again, either verbally, or mentally.*

Vocalizing or writing down the affirmative words works better than just thinking it silently. Writing the affirmative phrase is a particularly potent way of accomplishing the task of creating an affirmation. Writing brings muscle memory into play and leaves other parts of your brain free to achieve the next step.

Step 3: *While repeating the affirmative phrase, recall an emotionally potent memory or picture something in your mind such that it triggers the desired emotion.*

The emotion you want to trigger can be confidence or happiness or calmness. The goal here is to attach the triggering memory or thought and feeling on to the affirmative phrase. Once connected through classical conditioning every time you say your chosen phrase, you will feel whatever emotion you decided to attach to the words. For example, if you couple the phrase "I can do it" to the feeling of confidence, then you will experience that feeling every time you say the words. You can use memory or picture a mental image of you winning a competition to trigger the emotion confidence.

Step 4: *Repeat the steps two and three till the affirmative phrase and the memory become linked.*

You can stop repeating the process when merely repeating the phrase starts triggering an emotional response. This means that the memory and the sentence have become linked in your mind. Congratulate yourself on a job well done. You now have a powerful new affirmation to help you feel what you want when you want.

Base Technique 6: Peak-End Rule:

This rule is a heuristic that people use to judge the quality of life experiences. What are Heuristics? They are general rules of thumb which human beings use to make decisions and judgments, under uncertainty. In other words, it is the study of how decisions are made when the outcome of an action or the various factors affecting the issue are unclear. Most decisions are taken under conditions of uncertainty or when the amount of time we have to think things through is limited.
Heuristics form part of System 1 decision-making, what people sometimes call instinct. For the most part, our intuition serves us well. They allow us to make decisions quickly. They reduce the time and effort required to make decisions and simplify the process of decision-making.

According to studies, *people do not use the memory of a full event to assess how it went. They only use the Peak Emotional States and the End Emotional State to make value judgments.* Emotional State in this context can be happy, sad, angry, excited, etc. For example, you go on holiday, you have a great time for 3 days, but on the last day, you realize that you have lost your passport. Your assessment of the holiday now becomes almost entirely about the lost passport.

Your memory of the holiday has now been soured. Even though you did enjoy 3 good days, you are now far less likely to go back to the resort than if you had never lost the passport. The end assessment about how good or bad the event was, is an average of the strongest or Peak emotional experience and the End emotional experience. In the context of the holiday, end assessment is the average of the happiest or most exciting moments during the first 3 days and of how angry or annoyed you were at the time of leaving. The duration of the event is not relevant to this effect. In essence, whether it is a 3-hour meeting, a 4-day vacation, or your entire life, the heuristic is the same. Your mind only uses the most potent emotional moments, and the final situation when making judgments, this is called duration neglect.

You might be asking, why does this matter? At any time, how your unconscious Emotional-self feels about your life is based on the average of the most potent emotional memories from your whole life and your current feelings. When your unconscious Emotional-self looks at these few highs and lows and concludes, how it should feel about your life, it ignores the overwhelming majority of your life experiences.

Also, older memories fade in emotional strength. So, the really good or bad things that happened to you long ago are also not taken into account. The incorrect psychological assessments coming from the Peak-End process can lead to reckless decisions. The so-called "mid-life crisis" when people feel that they haven't done enough in their life, can partly be attributed to the mistakes of this heuristic. *You cannot change how your brain functions, but when your emotions tell you something, you should pause and think if they are telling you the truth.*

When trying to make a judgment about your life, you must take extra care. You should not forget all those not-so-high highs and not-so-low lows that form the majority of our lives. All those fun times with friends, that exam you scored high marks on, that time your boss praised you for a job well done, the times you made your partner laugh, they all count.

Your life isn't just the highs and lows, it is all those moments in between as well, remember them.

Base Technique 7: Memory Reinterpretation
What is Memory Reinterpretation? In simple terms, it is recalling a memory and then looking at it in a whole different way to change how you feel about it.

Memory Reinterpretation is something most people unknowingly practice and is critical to building a healthy mind in the long term. There is no way to live in our world and not be exposed to negativity. Relationships break up, loved ones die, jobs are lost, and sometimes bad things happen, that is life. Also, we, humans, don't always react well in stressful situations, leading to us doing things we later regret. We sometimes see things we would have preferred not to have seen and experience things we wish we didn't live through. Memory Reinterpretation (MR) is one way to neutralize bad memories. MR will also reduce the intensity of emotions like sadness, shame, embarrassment, resentment, regret, hate, etc. that arise from hurtful memories.

Even if you can't prevent negative experiences from occurring, how we interpret those memories, and how they influence us is still under our control. You can reinterpret what happened at a later time and remove the negative emotions attached to the memory of the event.

To construct a positive outlook on life in a world filled with negativity and build a positive sense of self, you will need to identify, analyze, and reinterpret negative memories.

Negative memories can be a cause of internal conflicts, anger, frustration, hatred, self-hatred, etc. How you can reinterpret specific memories depends on that particular instance. For instance, reinterpreting your memories of a break up is not the same as reinterpreting that of you embarrassing yourself in a competition.

All that said, *it is important to keep in mind that reinterpretation is not about altering the hard facts of memory but is about changing how you view them emotionally.*

A lot of people knowingly or unknowingly alter or suppress their memories to make them feel better. Many a time, the suppression or altering of a recollection is done automatically by the brain without the person being consciously aware of it. Knowingly or unknowingly suppressing your memories is not desirable as it can have many harmful effects. For one, it can lead to you repeating the mistakes that caused the bad experience. Secondly, it can cause misunderstanding with other people, which can bring all kinds of other problems in your life. Worst of all, suppressed memories can give rise to desires and emotions, without you understanding why you are feeling this way. Memory reinterpretation can be a way to address these issues.

Memory reinterpretation should always be about changing your perspective on an event to make it emotionally neutral. It should not be about trying to suppress the memory, or about reversing the emotions associated with a memory such as changing a negative experience to a positive one or vice versa. How to do reinterpretation is explained in the next section.

Base Technique 8: Overcoming Bad Memories

Let's begin by defining what bad memories are. Bad memories are memories of events which may trigger sadness, anger, fear, anxiety, embarrassment, etc. I am stating the obvious, right? Well, not entirely, there are memories of adverse events that do not trigger these emotions. For example, memory of something that happened 10-15 years ago is a lot weaker emotionally than newer memories. Memories of events from 10-15 years ago don't trigger as strong emotions as 5-year-old or a few month old memories.

Time reduces the emotional impact of specific memories. Apart from memories that fade, some memories stay with you for longer. These are usually memories of events that are connected to you more directly. The memory of you embarrassing yourself in front of your crush may still be as potent 20 years later.

The recollection of the same crush rejecting you, however, will lose relevance after a while. Of course, this is not the same with everyone or every incident. Some people have such high self-esteem that making a fool of themselves in front of others has no emotional impact on them.

The reason I am pointing all these things out is to show that the emotional impact of memory changes naturally over time. This is because every time you recall a memory, it is rerecorded. This is called Memory Reconsolidation. When you recall a bad memory, the experience of it is naturally less intense than when the event happened. The recollection is then rerecorded with the now less intense feelings. This process repeats each time you recall a memory. The strength of the emotions associated with an event progressively reduces over time, till the recollection becomes emotionally neutral. The memories that buck this trend are memories that are too painful, and people try to suppress those memories instead of fully recalling them.

Psychologists make use of the phenomenon of Memory Reconsolidation in Psychotherapy and one example is the so-called talking cures. This is also why people say talking about a problem helps, because every time you recall a memory, the emotional impact of the event usually decreases.

Why is it important to understand the mechanism underlying the "talking cure"? Well, because now that we know it, we can apply it ourselves and reduce the emotional impact of the memories quicker. Also, now that we understand the mechanism, we can do it without the help of costly professionals, friends, or relatives. It is always good to have emotional support but there are times in everyone's life when they have only themselves to rely on. Please do not misunderstand this to mean I am dissuading you from seeking help. However, the unfortunate truth is that for many people, good-quality emotional support is not available.

 Anyway, knowing all this, how do we reduce the emotional impact of bad memories? There are two ways to alter the emotions associated with a specific memory, namely Emotion Substitution and Memory Reinterpretation. We will start by looking at how the Emotion Substitution can be employed for this purpose.

Emotion Substitution Method of Memory alteration

Emotion substitution is a relatively easy way of changing the way you feel about someone, something, or an event. The following are the steps involved in the emotion substitution technique of altering the emotions attached to a memory.

Step 1: Trigger a counter-emotion by thinking an appropriate trigger-thought or by exposing yourself to a suitable external stimulus.

An example of how a negative or positive emotion can be triggered easily would be by playing music or by watching an emotionally potent movie scene. You can, of course, trigger emotion with another memory or mental picture as we discussed in the previous section on the Emotion Substitution technique. However, in Step 2, you are going to recall the memory you want to alter, so you might find triggering emotion with external stimulus more practical. That said if you personally find it easier to trigger a feeling with a trigger-thought, memory, or mental image, then that is fine too.

What stimuli will work for you depends entirely on your personality and the emotion you are trying to trigger. The type of stimulus I find positive or uplifting may not necessarily have the same impact on you. That said, soothing music makes you feel calm or uplifting music, which makes you feel happy or excited, especially of an instrumental nature is ideal. It is better to not use as trigger-stimuli music with lyrics, especially more extreme forms such as heavy metal or rap. The words of a song can have psychological connections that you may be unaware of, and this is why music with lyrics should be avoided as trigger-stimulus.

Apart from music, you also alter memories while watching movie scenes. A particularly funny or uplifting movie scene can trigger positive counter-emotions in you. The goal here is to trigger an emotion that is opposing to the sentiment you want to counter. If the memory you are trying to alter is sad, use happiness as the counter-emotion. If the recollection you wish to neutralize is a happy one, then use sadness as the counter-emotion.

Do not use unrelated emotions, for example, if you try to counter grief with faith or patriotism, then it won't work correctly. Unconnected emotions won't counter each other and will instead get coupled together through classical conditioning. This coupling of unrelated feelings can have unintended side effects. For example, if you attempt to counter sadness with belief or worship, which a lot of people do, all that will be accomplished is, both emotions will get attached. When faith in a specific ideology or religion, and grief get coupled together, it can manifest as extreme behavior.

Another way to trigger positive emotions is by simply smiling or laughing. Theories of Emotion in the field of psychology tell us that physical cues created by a feeling such as a smile also work in reverse. What does that mean?

If you smile, even without reason to do so, then your brain will release a jolt of happy chemicals into your bloodstream. This is one of the principles behind the laughter therapy. Hundreds of thousands of people around the world go to parks as a part of laughter clubs and practice fake laughing as a group because it makes them happier. So, if the other methods of triggering emotions don't work for you then just faking loud laughter or even smiling will trigger some positive feelings. The intensity of the happy feeling triggered will be proportional to the scale of your fake laugh.

Step 2: Recall the memory you wish to alter
Think about whatever you want to modify in its entirety, remember all aspects of it. Do not spend so much time on a recollection that the emotions from it start to build up and overwhelm the counter-emotion. The key here is to overwrite the feelings associated with the remembrance with new, less intense emotional information. If the original emotional state of the memory is reasserted, then the purpose of the technique is defeated, and the emotional intensity won't decrease. *One easy way to accomplish this is to recall bad memories while watching a video of your favorite jokes from a good comedy movie. The positive feelings from the film's humor will then counter and rewrite whatever pain used to be there.*

If you substituted the emotion and recalled the memory, then the recollection will be re-recorded by your brain, with the new emotional information. Therefore, only recollect a memory as long as your current emotional state is less intense than the emotions initially associated with the recollection.

Step 3: Perform another Emotion Substitution
Now it is time to wipe the memory out of your mind, by shifting your emotional attention to something else. Perform another Emotion Substitution so that you don't end up dwelling on the memory. Dwelling on the recollection can reinforce initial emotions, so it is best avoided. However, do not use the same stimulus, and instead use a different, preferably more potent trigger-stimulus. The trigger-stimulus can be some other strong positive memory or mental image that you find compelling. For example, you can remember some happy occasion with your child, romantic partner, sibling, parents, etc.

Repeat this process once or twice a day until the memory you wish to alter becomes emotionally neutral. How long it takes is entirely dependent on the initial emotional intensity of the recollection and the strength of the counter-emotion you used.

You don't need to try to make a memory completely emotionally neutral in one session, as this would be difficult. You should progressively reduce the emotional impact of the recollection over multiple sessions. Over time your ability to rewrite memories will improve. At the stage I am in, I can rewrite any memory in one go and with little effort.

Advisory: Please keep in mind the previous warnings regarding Emotion Substitution. Do not use the same stimulus over and over again as this will cause Classical Conditioning. In Steps 1 and 3 of each session, you should use different external stimuli or memories to trigger emotions. Using different stimuli will prevent Classical Conditioning from occurring.

Now, we move on to the second method for memory alteration that is Memory Reinterpretation.

Memory Reinterpretation Method of Memory Alteration

Memory Reinterpretation (MR) is the harder of the two techniques but is ultimately more beneficial. MR allows you not only emotionally neutralize an event but to completely change how you see it. You can also combine the Memory Reinterpretation and Emotion Substitution (ES), as you will see later.

Whenever possible, you should use MR or combined MR plus ES techniques. Only use pure Emotion Substitution if you cannot think of a way to reinterpret a memory. So, how do we achieve Memory Reinterpretation?

One way to change the way you see an event or person is to shift the focus of the memory from one part of the recollection to another. This technique utilizes the Peak-End rule, which we covered earlier in this chapter. The Peak-End Rule tells us that people judge events based on the highest and lowest emotional experiences and your emotional state at the end. So, Peak-End rule tells us that people do not look at the whole event when judging how good or bad something was, only the highs, lows, and the end. I will give you a small example from my own life, to demonstrate what I mean.

When I was about 14, I went to learn swimming during my summer school holidays. On the last day of the swimming class, there was a competition where the students competed against each other in various categories. The pool was an Olympic size swimming pool, and I was one of the older students in the class. Other kids my age and I were supposed to take a swan dive at the shallow end, and the first person to swim the whole length of the pool wins.

The problem was that I had missed the last week of classes because school had started again and so never learned how to swan dive. At the shallow end, the water was only about 2-3 feet deep, and the jumping-off point was at least 6 feet from the surface of the water. I was sure that had I tried to do a swan dive from that point, I would not be able to pull it off and would hit the bottom of the pool. I could have explained my fears to the instructors, and they would have understood, but for some reason, I did not. Instead, I went and took the standard starting position that you see in all the swimming competitions, with the hands touching feet. The instructors started the countdown, three, two, one, and standing there on the diving platform; I realized something. I knew I had no interest in risking busting my head on the pool floor merely to avoid embarrassment.

Then, the instructor said, go, and instead of doing a swan dive as the rest of the guys did, I just jumped down into the pool, feet first, and then started swimming. Everyone laughed, and I could hear their laughter. Unfortunately for me, as it turned out, my humiliation quotient for the day wasn't up yet. Now I don't know what you know about swimming but doing a swan dive gives you quite the head start in any swimming competition.

Since the other guys had done a swan dive and I had just jumped vertically down, they had quite the head start on me. I, though, am a fighter and don't like to lose, so I did the only thing I could do, I swam as hard as I could, and it worked. I started closing the distance, and I had almost reached the guy at the 3rd place when my luck ran out.

I was swimming so hard at one point that I did not get enough time to take a full breath. How did that happen? My head was shifting too fast between air and water; that is how. Anyway, the details aren't crucial to the point I am trying to make. The results were predictable. I was running out of breath.

To make matters worse, by this point, I was in the deep end of the pool. At the deepest end, the pool was 50ft deep, and I had just crossed the 40ft mark. Being me, I thought to myself, I am already at the last leg if I could just hold on for a minute more, then I can finish, and maybe I even win third place. Also, I thought, I am not in any real danger of drowning, with so many instructors watching on, so no need to worry. But then a point came when I could no longer ignore the burning in my lungs. Having messed up my rhythm, I had no breath left, and I was no Olympic swimmer, only a kid who had just learned to swim.

I did the only thing I could do, veered left, and swam towards the edge of the pool. Reaching the side just in time, I took in a lung full of air, and I have to say, what a relief it was merely to breathe again. You never appreciate the little things in life, like breathing, till you suddenly can't.

All the instructors came running asked me if I was ok and what happened. I said I am fine, explained everything, and yeah, it was all fine. Except, of course, everyone's opinion of me had taken a nosedive. Once the prize-giving ceremony and everything was over, we all headed back home. On the bus ride back, well again, the predictable happened, and I got made fun of and that too by much younger kids. When you are 14, getting laughed at by a bunch of 10-year-olds is a bit of a low point.

Now I will not go so far as to say this memory was the bane of my existence because it wasn't. I rarely thought about this incident. However, every now and then, when I had to do public speaking or something, I would think of this memory and cringe. I would remember this event when I thought of swimming or had to do something potentially embarrassing. I would recall how I felt in that situation, cringe, and then try to suppress this memory.

Eventually, I realized, rewriting this memory and making it emotionally neutral was a lot better way of dealing with it than swatting it away. I recognized that even though I was pushing it away from my conscious, it was still stuck in my unconscious. Buried in my psyche, it could possibly be impacting my overall confidence level, without me even realizing it.

Therefore at the age of 32, 21 years after the fact, I rewrote the memory. How I solved the problem was by refocusing the peak emotional point from me jumping and making a fool of myself to another part of the recollection. On the same day, on the bus ride back from the pool, when the other kids were making fun of me, my friends defended me. My friends got angry and told the kids mocking me to shut up. My friends coming to my defense was very emotionally satisfying for me. Let us face it, who doesn't like to know that there are people in your life who care about you enough to stand up for you.

When this memory popped up instead of pushing it away, I recalled the memory. I thought specifically about my friends defending me, I pictured it in mind, thus triggering an emotional response. Subsequently, when my brain rerecorded the memory, the emotional peak of the memory was no longer me embarrassing myself, but my friends defending me.

While this did not completely turn the recollection from a negative into a positive one, it did lead to the negative and the positive emotional peaks evening out. Shifting the peak and end emotional states of the memory made it more emotionally neutral. Now, the recollection was no longer about my failure and embarrassment but instead about people caring about me enough to stand up for me.

While the example I have given is relatively mild, worse memories can also be reinterpreted in this manner. Refocusing memories from the negative part on to a recollection of people supporting you or consoling you is very much possible. Whether the consoling happened that day, two days, or even a year later does not matter. In human memory, time is not an immutable variable as it is in the real world, so when the consoling happened is not as critical. It only matters that the consoling was related to the memory you are trying to modify. That said, too long a time differential can make the reinterpretation harder to achieve. For instance, if there is a gap of say ten years, between the event and the consoling, then you may find it harder to make it work.

The Peak-End rule states that how we recall an event depends more on the peak emotional moments and what we felt when the incident ended rather than on the entire experience. Refocus your attention on a different part of the memory such that it triggers intense counter-emotion. If you shift the emotional focus of the event, then recollection is rerecorded with a different interpretation, and that is how Memory Reinterpretation (MR) works. In the step by step format, the MR technique is as follows,

Step 1: Recall the memory

Step 2: Refocusing your attention on a different part of the recollection, preferably one with different emotional resonance.

Picture the new focal point of the memory in your mind till it triggers an emotional reaction. Subsequently, spend a minute or two ruminating about that part of the incident to allow the emotions to really register. Do not focus on any other part of the memory, or the effect will be diminished.

Step 3: Once you have finished refocusing, do an **Emotion Substitution** so that you don't end up dwelling on the memory.

Use different trigger-thoughts when doing Emotion Substitution to prevent Classical Conditioning.

Following these three steps will cause the memory to rerecord with the new emotional information. Repeat this process consciously once or twice a day, or every time the memory pops up until it becomes emotionally neutral.
You can also combine the Emotion Substitution (ES) and Memory Reinterpretation (MR) techniques to produce faster results. To merge the two methods, simply replace Step 2 of the ES with Step 2 of MR. The decision on whether or not to combine the two techniques I leave to you, as different people have different capabilities. The ability to recall memories, and analyze them, etc. varies from person to person, so which method will work for you depends on you.

Also, just because memory has been evened out emotionally doesn't necessarily mean that the effect it had on your behavior will completely disappear. Emotionally neutralizing the memories, however, does reduce the power that these learned rules will have in your life and will lead to these rules fading faster.

For example, memories of a bad break up do not have the same impact after five years as it did a month after the fact. That said, the effect bad memories have on your behavior lasts a lot longer than the recollection's emotional relevance.

Your unconscious Emotional-self learns and internalizes rules of conduct based on your life experiences. These life-experience derived behavioral rules become a part of your Instinctive Moral Code and drive your emotions. Someone who has gone through multiple breakups and has been emotionally hurt numerous times is likely to have a jaded attitude towards relationships and life in general.

A disheartened approach to life will have a negative impact, not just on their future romantic relationships but also on other relationships such as those with parents, friends, co-workers, etc. Depending on the level of hurt emotions a person carries with them, even the children of such individuals will be impacted by the behavioral impact of these memories.

However, as bad memories fade, you find it easier to do things like say, trust people, which at one point may have seemed impossible. The faster you neutralize bad memories, the quicker their effects on your behavior will fade.

The less affected your decisions are by emotional variances, the more likely you are to have a stable and positive life. Long term emotional equanimity can only be build by developing a high sense of meaning. But, these practical techniques will help you achieve higher emotional stability in the meantime.

Now we move on to the next chapter, which deals with situation-specific emotion control methods.

Chapter 2
Situation Specific Emotion Control

How to deal with Nervousness, Unwarranted Worrying, and Anxiety

A lot of people are very prone to worrying about the "What if" and then becoming anxious about hypothetical scenarios that usually never happen. The constant worrying and anxiety reduce the general quality of life of the worrying individual. The negative emotions make individuals more prone to health issues, both psychological and physical such as high blood pressure, obesity, substance abuse, depression, etc. The worrying individual transfers a lot of their negativity to the people around them, and this makes people less interested in being around worriers. Of course, people shunning you will never be something that is going to work out in your favor.

There are two things you need to do to deal with this issue. One is to reduce the emotional impact of previous negative life experiences using Memory Reinterpretation (MR) technique. As pointed out earlier, you should use MR or combined MR plus Emotion Substitution (ES) to make negative memories more emotionally neutral. Only use pure ES if a specific memory is too hard to reinterpret.

This will reduce your tendency to worry if your tendency to worry is being caused by previous bad memories. Of course, if the anxiety problem is genetic, which it often can be, then the problem will be harder to manage. Mind you, it could also be that the bad memories causing the issue are from your childhood, and you are not consciously aware of it. Childhood memories have a profound effect on behavior, but people are often less aware of them. If the problem memories hail from your childhood, then memory reinterpretation is all the more critical.

You can use self-awareness technique we talked about earlier to try and figure out if any particular memory is causing your tendency to worry. In the earlier example, we reinterpreted memory by focusing on a different part of it. There is another means which can be used to make memories more positive. We can change the way we see an event by comparing it with something worse and reminding ourselves that at least it wasn't that bad. This technique utilizes Simulation Heuristic.

Simulation Heuristic is the phenomenon where people's perception of the likelihood of an event changes based on how easily they can picture it in their mind. This heuristic doesn't just come into play when people try to figure out what sequence of events is more likely in the future.

Simulation heuristic also impacts your perception of what you could have done differently in the past.

In an experiment, researchers told participants about a fictitious incident. Two people were supposed to leave town on the same day by two different flights. They both left town in the same car, but got stuck in traffic and missed their flights. Upon arrival at the airport, one person was informed that his plane left on time about half an hour ago. The other individual was told that his flight was delayed and he missed it by just 5 mins. Researchers then asked the participants to guess which of the two people was more upset. Unsurprisingly, 96% of the participants answered that the second person would have been more troubled.

This, even though the end result in both cases is the same, aka the individuals missed their flight. Generically speaking, this happens because, when it is easier for someone to imagine an alternate chain of events with a better outcome, then they are more likely to develop regrets. In the case of the second person, just by altering one or two decisions, he could have saved 5 mins and thus caught the flight.

Since the outcome of the incident could have been different with so few alterations, the second person would be able to imagine alternate scenarios more quickly. This would increase his feeling of being hard done by fate, and hence, he would feel more regret. Whereas in the case of the first person, it is harder to imagine what he could have done differently to shave 30 mins off his arrival time. The alternate world where the first person made his flight is thus harder to imagine. Therefore the first person would experience less regret.

What can we learn from this that will be of use in our everyday life? Well, an important thing to know is, imagining better scenarios after something negative happened will make you feel worse about it. **Deconstructing events and realizing where you went wrong is critical to avoiding future mistakes.** Imagining or focusing on better outcomes, however, does not give you new insights.

If you must analyze an adverse event, then before doing it, imagine a worse scenario. Explicitly picture in your mind a worse sequence of events and show yourself how you are lucky things didn't go that way.

Using this tactic will help you obtain an entirely different perspective on any adverse event.

Repeatedly visualizing better outcomes that you failed to achieve will, in the long run, lead to loss of confidence, motivation, etc. After neutralizing the negative emotions attached to an event, you will be able to analyze it more accurately.

Studies show that Simulation heuristic has also been shown to be a significant contributor to clinical anxiety disorders. More imaginative individuals have a higher chance of developing anxiety-related issues. This is because it is easier for such individuals to visualize negative scenarios in their mind, such as accidents, diseases, etc. Picturing positive events can be helpful, but that tactic may not work for everyone.

The way to combat this is to imagine worse scenarios instead of better ones. You can then point out to yourself that at least it wasn't as bad as it could have been. When constructing worse case scenarios, you shouldn't compare yourself to other people, but should instead imagine situations where things could have been worse. The key here is to picture a worst-case scenario in your mind, and not just tell yourself it could have been worse. Mentally visualize a worst-case scenario in such a way that it triggers an emotional response. It is the emotional response that leads to the memory being reinterpreted, not the rational thought.

Memory formation is performed by the unconscious, not the conscious. *So, if you want to alter how you perceive an event, you have to talk in a language that your unconscious Emotional-self understands, namely that of emotions.*

For instantaneous relief from anxiety, Emotion Substitution (ES) is the best option. Simply picture something that is emotionally potent in your mind and at least for a little while your worries will subside. To know the exact methodology for ES refer back to the section on it. However, this is not a permanent solution as the anxieties will in all likelihood return in a little while. Memory Reinterpretation is the only way to address the issue more permanently.

Repeating Affirmations that are emotionally potent over and over again is another way to address the issue. If there is a phrase that is emotionally potent for you, then you can use that. You can also create a Personalized Affirmation using the method described in the relevant section.

For example, if you experience stage fright or are anxious about an interview, you can picture in your mind an incident where you wowed people or succeeded in some fashion.

You can then repeat a phrase like "I am awesome" or "I can do it," while maintaining the positive mental image, thus creating a personal affirmation. You can then repeat the phrase as many times as necessary to make yourself feel better in the moment and tackle anxiety. However, do not recite an affirmation phrase too many times, too fast as it will lose emotional relevance. Here again, the key is not the phrase being repeated but rather about triggering a strong enough emotion to counter the anxiety you are experiencing. This method makes it easier to carry out emotion substitution without actually having to visualize a mental image each time.

Next, we move on to another problem most people face at one time or another. The problem is that of being attracted to people who either do not feel the same way or are individuals who we shouldn't be interested in, such as co-workers.

How to stop yourself from being attracted to someone
At some point, most people find themselves interested in someone who is out of bounds or does not reciprocate your feelings. There are also environments where romantic entanglements are best avoided.

Unfortunately, natural human biological drives do not work that way, they do not recognize the difference between socially appropriate and inappropriate. The following are some techniques that will help you control your sex drive and not to be attracted to people with whom you have no future.

The "last fight" method
The base techniques used here are Classical Conditioning, Operant Conditioning, and Emotion Substitution. What is the last fight method? Whenever you feel attraction towards someone that you do not wish to be attracted to, at that moment, picture in your mind the last fight you had with an ex. The argument doesn't necessarily have to be the last one, but it should be one that was emotionally painful to you. This is because stronger the negative emotion attached with the memory, the quicker you will be able to get rid of your attraction for said person.
Now if merely picturing isn't enough, then you can go the extra mile and do the next step as well. Instead of only visualizing a fight with your ex, in your mental image, replace your ex with the person you attempting not to be attracted towards. So, now the mental picture must be of you being hurt by that person, the attraction to whom you are trying to neutralize.

You must use the Last Fight method whenever the memory of the person you are attracted to comes up in your mind or whenever you see the person. Repeat till you entirely stop being drawn to the subject of your attraction. It will not take more than two or three repetitions for you to lose your interest in the person. Following is the Last Fight technique in the step by step format,

Step 1: Whenever you think of or see your crush then at that time recollect a particularly hurtful fight you had with your ex. You can also use an argument with someone you had romantic feelings for but who spurned your affection and mistreated you. Using different negative memories each time you use the method will produce better results than using the same negative incident.

Step 2: Remember the fight in such a way that it triggers a strong negative emotional response. However, instead of recalling the argument as one between you and an ex-partner, imagine you fought with the crush.

Step 3: Repeat this process until you stop being attracted to that person and no longer wish to see them. It will not take long.

I have used the word crush in a couple of places, but it doesn't necessarily have to be a crush.

The technique will work for any person you are trying not to be attracted to, irrespective of the strength of attraction. When you use this technique, multiple things happen in your brain. One is Operant conditioning. Your unconscious will quickly realize that feeling positive emotions about the person will immediately trigger negative feelings. Your unconscious Emotional-self will then avoid thinking about the person to avoid feeling bad. Second, each time you use the Last Fight Method, your unconscious will transfer the negative feelings you have for your ex on to your crush. With every use of this technique, you will become less interested in the person, and after 2-3 times, you will entirely lose interest.

The Revulsion Method
This technique is for people who may not want to remember uncomfortable fights or for some other reason, do not want to use the Last Fight technique. The Revulsion Method is similar to the previous method in terms of base techniques but uses different emotions.

In the previous method, we used sadness, discomfort, irritation, and other similar emotions, arising out of a fight, to replace attraction. In this technique, we will instead use a mental image that triggers the feeling of disgust.

Disgust is an emotion that exists with the explicit purpose of making you feel repulsed by anything that may be unhealthy or harmful to you. In that sense, the feeling of disgust is ideal for Emotion Substitution here because it has the least amounts of connections to other emotions. That is to say, disgust does not transform into another feeling. For example, sadness can escalate to depression, irritation can grow into anger, but disgust just remains the same.

In a step by step format, the technique is as follows,

Step 1: *Whenever you think of or see the person who you don't want to be attracted to, at that time, picture in your mind something that disgusts you.* For example, you can visualize putrefying food, a corpse, or anything that genuinely repulses you. I am purposefully avoiding giving truly disgusting examples to avoid making you feel revolted. You can also recollect a memory of which triggered in you the feeling of disgust.

Step 2: Repeat this process until you no longer feel attracted to the person. If it is merely an attraction, it will not take more than 2 or 3 attempts for the feeling to dissipate.

Advisory: If you use a mental image that you find strongly disgusting, then you might end up feeling a slight vomit reflex whenever you see the person. You do not want that if this is a person you will be regularly seeing. Therefore to start with, use a mental image that you find mildly disgusting. Escalate to a highly disgusting mental picture only if the milder stimulus didn't do the trick.

There is one more thing you should know about these techniques. There are two different ways in which you can use both Last fight method and Revulsion Method. One, if you use the same memory or mental image multiple times, then Classical Conditioning will occur. The memory you used will be attached by your mind to your crush. If a negative feeling is firmly attached to this person, it will make it harder for you to change your mind later if the situation changes.

Two, you can use different memories or mental images each time. If you do that, then Classical Conditioning or permanent attachment will not occur, but it will still work, as Operant Conditioning will happen. Your unconscious will understand that this person is not suitable for you and will not dwell on this person anymore. However, Operant Conditioning is not permanent and fades with time so the attraction can be rekindled later if you so wish.

How to get over a Relationship or Crush

Most people, at one point or another, have faced this situation. Whether it is a broken relationship, a case of unrequited love or particularly bad crush, it happens. After a relationship failure, we are left with the need to get over a relationship that we thought was going to last forever and get back to some semblance of a healthy life. How do we get over our feeling? Is there some scientific blueprint on how to get over a relationship? Maybe a well thought out way using which we can move on? If there is such a blueprint I have never found it and so I came up with one of my own.

If you were in a serious, emotionally dependent relationship, then when it breaks off, there are four problems you can experience. The four issues will vary in intensity depending on the duration and emotional dependence you had on your now broken romance. The four difficulties are as follows,

I.   All of a sudden, there is a hole in your life. A lot of time and energy that you previously expended on your partner is now free, and you don't know what to do with yourself. All the free time and energy is where the empty mind is the devil's workshop concept comes in.

When you have a lot of free time, you keep trying to figure out what to do with yourself. This pondering of what to do then inevitably leads to memories of you and your ex spending time together. Dwelling on memories of you and your ex will cause emotional pain and will trigger a sense of hopelessness. The despair will make you feel that your life will always be incomplete without your ex.

II.   You had a vision for your life that included this person. Now, without that person, the long-term vision for your life has become suddenly incomplete, or worse completely impractical. The state of confusion where you have no life plan can be highly uncomfortable for your unconscious. Your unconscious then tries to solve this lost state of uncertainty by reaching for the familiar, specifically by making you want to get back together with your ex.

III.   You had a lot of emotions attached to your ex, and there was an emotional high that you got from your relationship. Emotional high doesn't necessarily have to be positive but can also be from negative feelings. Depending on how long and emotionally intense the relationship was, the result of the sudden disappearance of those emotions can be very similar to the withdrawal symptoms of a drug addict.

Just as withdrawal symptoms drive drug addicts to take drugs again, you will also feel compelled to contact your ex.

IV.   The fourth problem is our drive to figure what went wrong or what we did wrong, and all the negative emotions that come with those questions. The feelings of sadness, regret, worthlessness, hopelessness, emptiness that you feel as you sit at home unable to come up with a satisfactory answer. The questions of how everything went to hell, how this happened, etc. might seem like critical questions, but they rarely have clear cut answers.

Your apparent inability to understand what happened will also drive you to seek out contact with your ex to make sense of what happened. Unfortunately, in most cases, no one thing leads to relationship failures, a great many factors play a role in such situations. Human behavior is complex, and most people are unaware of their insecurities, complexes, and drives. It is highly unlikely your ex will be willing, or even self-aware enough, to be able to give an answer that will satisfy your emotional needs. In the long run, finding out why a relationship failed is a good idea, but in short to medium term, you will be too emotionally close to the problem to analyze it objectively.

Therefore, trying to figure out the reasons for why a relationship failed, a day or two or even a month after the event, will not yield any rational insightful answers.

These four problems together account for the emotional upheaval, the desire to get back together and the "missing your ex" that you might have experienced post-breakup. The methods to solve these problems can be categorized into two components. First is the fixing the practical issues, such as those of having a lot of free time and energy, constructing a vision for your life independent of your ex, etc. Second is dealing with the emotional problems generated by the break up as well as getting rid of the romantic feelings you have for your ex.

Phase 1: Dealing with Emotional Issues
While I am framing this is as Phase 1 and 2, these are steps that you should take concurrently not one after the other. Practical problems drive emotional issues, and emotional difficulties will hinder your efforts to deal with the real-world obstacles. Both practical and emotional challenges, therefore, need to be addressed simultaneously.

Technique 1: Something that often happens post-breakup is that you will find yourself thinking of you ex, which is only natural, given the 4 problems we talked about earlier. *You cannot move on with your life if your Emotional-self continues to bring up memories of your ex or your relationship.* The following method is essentially the same as the Last Fight Method we talked in the previous section. Here again, we use the base technique of Operant Conditioning to convince your unconscious Emotional-self to stop thinking about things that hurt you.

Step 1: Whenever you think of your ex or a related memory, recollect a particularly bad fight you had with your ex. Remind yourself of a specific memory where your ex mistreated you or emotionally hurt you in some manner. Whether your ex broke up with you or if you broke up with your ex, odds are there are bad memories you can use for this purpose.

Step 2: Remember the hurtful memory in such a way that it triggers a negative emotional response. The negative emotion is the key to making the technique work. The negative emotions triggered by the memory act much like taking away video games from a child for misbehaving.

It tells the unconscious that doing that action, whether it is not studying or thinking about your ex, will cause adverse outcomes and hence should be avoided.

Step 3: Repeat this process until your unconscious Emotional-self stops bringing up memories or thoughts regarding your ex. It will not take long.

Technique 2: You can speed up the process of getting over someone, by actively reinterpreting memories instead of waiting for your unconscious to bring up these memories. This technique uses a combination of base techniques of Emotion Substitution and Memory Reinterpretation. As we learned from examining the Peak-End rule in Chapter 4, you do not need to alter every memory to change your remembering self's perception of something.

When enough positive memories from your relationship have been turned into emotionally neutral ones, then your perception of the entire relationship will change. *Even if you were together for say 10 years, and your view of the relationship is significantly positive, just altering 6 or 7 key memories will change your feelings.* If the thought of emotionally neutralizing positive memories is upsetting to you, that is understandable.

However, you do keep in mind these memories will become emotionally neutral over time. This process will happen if you do nothing or something, just the time it takes will vary.

Additionally, this is the same process that Psychotherapists use in the so-called Talking Cures. All you are doing here is shortening the time frame required for the memories to become emotionally neutral. Under normal conditions, it takes many months or even years for your memories to become emotionally neutral. With this technique, depending on how you practice it, it will only take a week or two to neutralize memories and thus get over the relationship.

While there are no dangers with this technique, I would say, don't use this technique unless you have to. Only use this method if you experience severe distress post break up and are afraid you could slip into depression or resort to substance abuse. *I do not personally consider actively neutralizing positive memories to be a good thing, but it is better than depression, self-harm, alcoholism, etc.*

Refer back to the section on memory alteration to look up the exact step by step process involved in this technique.

Technique 3: This is a way to reinterpret your memories or relationship as a whole to make it easier for you to move on. Think of your ex, not as the person you loved, but as an entirely new person. Every time a thought of your ex comes up, think of your ex as someone who is no longer in this world. You should tell yourself that the person you loved is gone and can never be brought back. This is technically true because even if you get back together, you will never again be able to look at that person the same way. You will forever view your ex as someone who hurt you and therefore will always trust the person less. Because of these reasons, no matter what happens after a break-up, the person you loved before is truly gone and can never ever be brought back.

The key here is to feel the person as truly gone. It is not about merely saying to yourself verbally that the person is gone, but you must generate the appropriate feelings. Always keep in mind when trying to convince your unconscious emotional-self of anything, it is about repetition and emotions, not words.

Phase 2: Dealing with Practical Problems.

People have a tendency to try and fill the hole in their life left by the ending relationship with hobbies or with rebound relationships.

Hobbies are rarely satisfying enough to replace the emotional high you got from spending time with your partner. As for rebound relationships, research shows that the results of such relationships vary and depend on how emotionally satisfying the relationship is. If a person's experience with the rebound relationship is unsatisfying, it can even lead to a strengthening of their feelings for their ex. In my experience, both personally and from talking with people from many different countries, rebound relationships do often help people fill the emotional void in short-term. However, after a while, rebound relationships leave people feeling hollow and empty and regretting the experience to one extent or another.

The main reason most people regret their rebound relationships is that they often end with the other person getting hurt. What usually happens is that the other person becomes too attached and the person coming off of a break-up is unable to reciprocate. This mismatch in expectations then leads to another bad break up. There is a high probability that in your rush to make yourself feel better, you could end up hurting another person. Said person then has their own rebound and emotionally injures another person so on and so forth.

If everyone has at some point been hurt badly by a romantic partner, then they will inevitably go into the next romance with one foot firmly planted outside. After all, if you can be hurt once by someone you trust, then it can definitely happen again.

Within the context of relationships, marriages, family, etc. where implicit trust is key to long term success, having one foot out will definitely increase the rate of failure. In the long run, break ups, hook-ups, rebound relationships, etc. fundamentally undermine the social trust in which all romantic relationships are based. Trust between two people once lost is hard enough to reconstruct, near impossible even. So you can imagine how hard it would be to rebuild collective social trust in romantic relationships, marriage, etc. once that trust has been lost. The family unit is the building block of society, if the family weakens, the nation will soon follow. This cycle of break-ups and rebounds in this way impacts all people and relationships in societies where such behavior is prevalent.

The solution to the problems of decreased emotional stimulation and the increased free time and energy after a break-up is therefore not hobbies or rebound relationships.

The answer is to figure out, which core values you are passionate about and to recommit yourself to those values wholeheartedly and thus achieve meaning in your life. There are seven core values, that human beings value namely Knowledge, Beauty, Service, Faith, Excellence, Discipline, and Wisdom. How you can commit yourself to those core values and achieve meaning in your life is covered in detail in the next book in the series.

For me personally, committing myself to the Path of Service or helping others was what kept me going even when I was drowning in depression, suicidal thoughts, etc. In your case, if you are intellectual, then your path could be knowledge or wisdom. If you have an artistic temperament, then it could be beauty. If you are a competitive person, then your Path in Life could be excellence, etc. You can utilize the self-awareness technique described at the beginning of this chapter to figure which paths speak to you on a personal level. The key to overcoming emotional body blows such as break up, or a divorce, or a job loss lies in two things. One is having an identity that is not dependent on outside factors. The second is pursuing a life of meaning instead of pursuing chemical happiness or pleasure.

A combination of pursuing meaning in life and emotion management techniques will allow you to get over relationship break-up in short order, without damaging your sense of self.

How to deal with loss of a loved one

Dealing with the loss of a loved one is a lot similar to dealing with the breakup of an intense romantic relationship. The critical difference between death and breakup is the finality of death. With breakups, there is always the possibility, however faint, of rekindling the romance.
Just like in breakups, with a loss also, the challenge is not to dwell on what is lost. However, in the case of a death, spending a few days or a week or two mourning is appropriate. This is because if you use techniques to get over the loss of a loved one too quickly, you could end up feeling guilty about it later. Spending more than a week or two in mourning is not advisable because you could easily slip into depression.

So, what techniques do you use? Well, it depends on what role the individual played in your life. The more your life used to revolve around the lost person, the harder the loss will be on you.

The loss of a child, spouse, sibling, or parent tends to be the most severe losses a person can experience. The lack of purpose is what leads people to commit suicide after the loss of a loved one. A lot of parents commit suicide after a child passes away because they feel lost. They don't know how to live without the central purpose that children often are in parents' lives.

How to regain direction in your life or build meaning independent of other people is covered in the next book in the series. Building meaning in your life is an involved process, it is not a topic you can do justice to in a few paragraphs. The next book in the series will be out a few months after this book, so you can check it out then. For now, just know you should look for things that you find meaningful and pursue it. What people find meaningful varies from person to person. Some might find helping others worthwhile, for others, it might be protecting the environment, seeking knowledge, spirituality, art, etc. What you find meaningful depends on the kind of person you are.

Building meaning is, however, a long-term process. In the short term, you can use Contextualization, Emotion Substitution, and Memory Alteration.

Contextualization Technique

Step 1: Take a deep breath

Step 2: The first step to apply is Emotion Substitution (ES) because to think straight, you must be at least a little stable. For exactly how to use ES refer back to Chapter 1. When doing ES, DO NOT use any memory about your lost loved one. *In particular, do not dwell on any positive memories of the lost person because that will just make you yearn for their company.* You can use as trigger-thoughts memories of other people you care about. Pick a trigger-thought that counters your sadness and brings you to a state of stability so that you can engage in step 2.

Step 3: The second step is Contextualization. It is about viewing your loss in the broader context to bring yourself to peace with what has happened. You must contextualize loss, to be able to move on. You must come to terms with what it signifies. This can vary wildly depending on whom you lost, and the circumstance under which the loss happened. In other words, the context of the loss matters when contextualizing. We discussed this in the last Chapter as Base technique 9. The narrative we discussed in Base Technique 9 is the one I use, but if that doesn't work for you, you can use another.

If you are a firm believer in one religion, then you might have preferred narrative of your own already.

A sudden loss from disease or accident is often the hardest because you are not able to say goodbye in your mind. As long as you have an answer that satisfies you about "why bad things happen to good people," then that is what matters. My response, well, to me *all life and non-life is one, and all things in the Universe are one.*

Life is a part of the journey the cosmos is on from creation to destruction, to recreation. Your life, my life, the life of your loved ones is a part of the path of the Universe. In death, life returns back to the Universe from whence it came. Life and creation cannot exist without death and destruction. When we eat we destroy, even plants destroy matter in one state and recreate it in another. If nothing and no one ever died, life would quickly become untenable. So why do bad things happen? Because for one, what we think of as terrible is simply a natural cycle of creation, destruction, and recreation. Nothing is ever completely destroyed. We are all energy, all matter is energy, we were a part of the Universe in life, and we are a part of it in death. Life simply changes form from one form of existence to another. Nothing I have said here thus far is unscientific. All concepts stated here are scientifically proven facts.

Every time you find yourself feeling sad for those who have passed on, you must think about the broader context. You should remind yourself that nothing is ever truly gone. Think about how everything returns to the Universe from whence it came and picture the beauty of creation in your mind till you feel calm.

The beauty of nature cannot exist without the cycle of life, and death, visualize yourself as a part of that beauty till you feel the weight in your chest lessening.

If you feel the heaviness in your chest increasing, then stop, do an Emotion Substitution, and repeat Step 1-3 at a later time.

The key to convincing your unconscious Emotional-self is repetition and emotional potency. Repeat step 1-3 whenever you find yourself dwelling on sad thoughts until you feel the sadness decreasing. You are unlikely to feel entirely happy the first time you apply Steps 1-3, the process is incremental. Depending on how close you were to the person, the decrease in sorrow will happen in smaller increments. Each time you perform this, you will feel more at ease, but complete relief will take time.

Memory Alteration Method

You may or may not need to use this technique. Do this only if contextualization does not bring you any relief even after a week.
If training your unconscious to view your loss in the broader context isn't enough, then you need to address the thoughts that drive you to dwell on the lost loved one.

The memories could be possible hopes and dreams that you had for and with this person. If the lost loved one is your child, spouse, partner, sibling, friend, or parent, if you were close, then you probably had some plans together. These plans or hopes are probably emotionally potent for you, and maybe things that you did together always or dreams for the future. I do not write this lightly, but those dreams and memories need to become emotionally neutral. Saying hopes and dream need to be emotionally neutralized might seem heartless, but the loss of a loved one leads a lot of people to suicide. I can say with fair certainty that the person you cared about wouldn't want you to harm yourself. If other techniques don't work and even after a few weeks and you are as sad as ever, then memory alteration may be necessary.
How to reduce emotions associated with a thought or memory is described in Chapter 1, refer to the relevant section for details.

Now, we move on to the next technique.

How to rejuvenate your Feelings towards your Spouse or Long-term partner

Problems faced in long-term committed relationships and marriages can be myriad. The issues, however, can be divided into two categories Emotional and Practical. People usually try to solve the practical problems such as failure to communicate, and then hope that the negative emotions go away automatically afterward. As we have seen from our discussion thus far, that is not how emotions or the unconscious Emotional-self works.
Negative memories and emotions can hinder a person's desire to communicate openly and honestly. Negative emotions, therefore, do create functional problems and can also demotivate you from trying to resolve the issues that impact the relationship. It is consequently vital to address the negative emotions and practical difficulties simultaneously. The technique provided here, therefore, works to change the way you feel about your marital life.

According to Peak-End rule, how your Emotional-self feels about your marriage depends on the most intense emotional moments and the current state of your relationship.

Every experience you have during your matrimony does not factor into your feelings. What does that mean? As long as your unconscious Emotional-self remembers more positive memories than negative ones, your feelings about your marriage will be positive.

When the number and intensity of negative memories outstrip the positive experiences, then your feelings towards your marital life become negative. The negative memories may not necessarily stem from your marriage and can be deaths in the family, illness, financial issues, etc. However, more intense the bad memories, the worse will be your perception of your life. Additionally, as your marriage grows older, then past positive experiences can automatically lose emotional potency because of how human memory works. The combination of waning strength of old positive memories and growing negative memories can weaken long-term relationships. If you are someone in such an emotional state, then this technique could help you.

The basic principles behind this technique are Memory Reinterpretation and Emotion Substitution. There are two aspects to changing the way you feel about your marriage. First is neutralizing the negative memories, and the second is rejuvenating the positive memories.

How to emotionally neutralize negative memories is covered in the section on how to deal with bad memories. In this section, we will look into how you can revive fading positive memories only.

Rejuvenating Fading Positive Memories

Step 1: Identify the memories which used to hold the most meaning for you, for instance, your positive memories of your marriage. Focus on good memories of you and your partner. They can also be memories of when your partner helped you through a difficult time.

Step 2: Create an environment that triggers romantic emotions in you. You can achieve this in whatever way suits you. Romantic music, movies, etc. can work to trigger romantic feelings.

Step 3: Write down previously identified memories using a pen and paper while in a romantic mood. Cover at least two different incidents during each session. You should spend between 20-30 mins remembering and writing positive recollections each time you do this.
Writing your memories down works on the same principle as when your teachers made you write stuff over and over again as punishment when you were a kid.

Writing something triggers muscle memory and visual memory in addition to the standard memory processes and thus strengthens the recollection. When remembering and writing about an event, say your wedding day, focus on the aspects that made you particularly happy or excited. Take care not to let your mind wander into the problems affecting your relationship today. Keep your thoughts focused on the event you are recollecting, the specifics of that day, and most importantly, focus on your feelings for your partner at that time.

Step 4: Repeat this process every couple of days with different memories, with as many as positive memories as possible. Write each memory 2-3 times to reinforce it, but do not do it more than that as the emotional effects can fade. If you are writing a memory that you have already written down once then do it only after a gap of 1 week.

If you plan to write a memory a third time, then do it only after a gap of at least 2 weeks from the 2nd attempt. This is to prevent the creation of a predictable pattern, which can reduce their emotional impact. The goal here is to increase the emotional potency of the positive memories, and not to accidentally lessen their impact.

The increasing emotional potency of positive memories and decreasing strength of negative ones will reduce the bad feelings you may have towards your marital life. As the positivity that you have towards your marriage and partner grows, you will find it easier to address the practical issues that plague your relationship.

Create and Use an Affirmation
Another means through which you can improve your relationship stability is to create an affirmation that can quickly trigger positive emotions you have for each other. You can use an affirmative statement even in the middle of an argument to calm yourself down. For example, you can use a phrase such as "he/she loves me" as an affirmation. Whenever you feel yourself getting angry, you can use an affirmative expression to remind yourself that your partner loves you. If both people do this, then it can go a long way in reducing arguments and facilitating calm, honest, and productive conversations.

The technique for creating personalized emotionally potent affirmations has already been discussed in an earlier section. Please refer back to that section for the specifics on how to do it.

How to avoid hating people with different political and ideological opinions

One of the rising problems of today is the polarization that is growing in societies of democratic countries. The divisions are in large part due to an increasingly acidic political discourse and social media outrage culture. Mainstream media trying desperately to compete with digital platforms is adding further fuel to this fire.

Does this sequence of events sound familiar to you? Media outlets put out articles along established ideological and political lines saying there is a controversy. Supporters of various political and ideological groups then comment on those articles on Twitter, Facebook, etc. and engage in highly heated debates. Often these arguments involve threats, foul language, insults directed at your parents, etc. In some countries, the tribal divisions have become so toxic that people are carrying their quarrels from social media into the real world. People are ganging up and trying to get other people fired or evicted from their homes, etc. Social media mobs act out because they consider people with different opinions as evil.

This kind of tribalism can overtime rip nations apart, so it is in no one's best interest.

If the people of a country are too divided, then they cannot cooperate peacefully for the benefit of all. Therefore to address this issue of political division, this is an easy to implement technique based on the Peak-End rule.

Just after you finish arguing with someone or reading an article that is critical of the opposing side, take a moment and think of one positive thing about the people from the rival group. Remember the thought should trigger positive emotions, and merely thinking will not do the trick.

Human memory prioritizes the emotional peaks and emotional end state when forming judgments. So, if your final thought after an argument was something positive, then it will prevent your opinion of your political opponents from becoming hateful. Even if your view of an opposing group is already low, you can still practice this technique. Overtime your feelings towards the rival group will become less hateful if you do this exercise.
Please keep in mind, you are not doing this for anyone else's benefit. Hate, anger, and tribalism are not beneficial to your personal wellbeing or to the stability of the country where you live. Forgiving people makes you happier, so you are doing this for your sake and that of all the people you care about.

How to Motivate Yourself (for those who have trouble completing tasks)

This method is for any person who has trouble getting motivated. It will be most useful for people who suffered from long-term depression, but it will work for anyone.

Here we will apply the techniques we just learned about how to negotiate with your Emotional-self. When I went through long-term depression, which lasted over 7 years, I could not get anything done. I just didn't want to do it. I did not get any pleasure out of anything, and the world was either wholly bland or outright painful to me. Even after I came out of depression and was no longer suicidal, I just could not get myself to do anything. I did not experience pleasure, and the reward systems of my brain seemed to work in reverse. I had been depressed for so long that I experienced a desire to be unhappy than to be happy. This desire to be unhappy is something we commonly refer to as self-destructive tendencies.

In my case, the method I came up with was a little bit involved and did not produce consistent results. More recently, however, I came up with a technique to motivate myself that was simpler and produced longer-lasting results.

The key to the method is to break any task down into smaller tasks, and then rewarding yourself separately for completing each minor task.

For example, if I had a report to write, I would break it down into 200 words pieces. Every time I finished 200 words, I gave myself a piece of chocolate. In the beginning, I had to do this regularly, but as I went on, I found that I had less and less need for such motivation.

Chocolate worked for me, it could be something entirely different for you. Ultimately it is about taking up a task, breaking it up into smaller tasks and rewarding yourself when you complete them. As you complete more jobs or chores, you will require even less immediate reward. Over time you will be able to delay gratification enough to take on more challenging tasks. However, proceed slowly allow yourself to complete smaller tasks and gain confidence before progressing to more challenging tasks.

For example, you can increase the quantum of words from 200 to 400, then to 800, and so on. If you find yourself having motivation problems at any points, then come back down to a smaller number of words. There are no set schedules here, but instead, it is about what works for you.

What we want is for you to be able to motivate yourself to do the jobs you need to do, to succeed in life. If you follow this method and proceed gradually, then even someone who has suffered long-term depression should be able to restore functionality to their life. It worked for me, so it should work for you too.

Now, we move to Chapter 3, which features advanced Emotional Management Methods.

Chapter 3
Overall Emotional Management

How to improve your overall Emotional Control

This section will cover techniques that will allow you to achieve greater emotional control both in the moment and in the long term. In the first chapter, we talked about training our emotional control "muscles." This section is where we look at precise practical techniques that will help you do that.

You train yourself to control your emotions the same way you make yourself capable of running faster or lifting heavier weights, by actually doing it. As with all training, you should start with easier exercises and then working your way towards more difficult ones. In practical terms, you train your unconscious in phases, one set of techniques after the other.

This section contains a set of exercises where you try to bring your emotions under control in more and more challenging circumstances. There are 5 exercises, and each one is more difficult than the previous. The conditions under which you practice emotion-control can range from listening to music to riding a rollercoaster.

Do these exercises every once in a while to strengthen your emotion-control "muscles." You do not have to control your emotions every time you listen to music or watch a scary movie. These are like any physical exercise, practice them occasionally till you get the desired result. As you successfully complete each training exercise, your ability to control unexpected emotions like anger, anxiety, food cravings, sexual arousal, etc. will increase.

Exercise 1: Train yourself to remain emotionally neutral while listening to music
This might seem like a relatively easy task but is harder than it might seem at first glance. Also, this is just a starting point; the next phases will be even more difficult. Remember just like at the gym, here too, you should start small with the exercises and work your way up.

Step 1: Watch music videos, or listen to music that has an emotional impact on you. The emotion being triggered can be enjoyment, excitement, romance, etc. but it can also be frustration, anger, irritation, annoyance, etc. The key here is to train yourself to control your emotions better. However, if there is a particular emotion that you are having a difficult time controlling, then you can focus on songs that trigger that emotion.

Listen to the song for a bit, at least until it triggers requisite emotions before moving on to the next step. Listen to at least 2 songs during each session. Each session will, therefore, take less than 10 minutes. Play different songs during each session.

Step 2: Take a deep breath, try to focus inwards and visualize your breath as a column of light traveling down your throat and filling your chest. Focus on that light, let it fill your chest, now let go and "watch" as that light leaves you. Repeat this process 3-5 times till you start to feel more emotionally neutral. This step is to allow you to center yourself before trying to shift your focus. As you become more proficient at controlling your emotions, this step will become unnecessary.

Step 3: Now that you have centered yourself. Try to think of something else. During early sessions, you can think of something that is emotionally dissonant to whatever emotion is being triggered by the music. For example, if the music is making you irritated or angry, then think of something that makes you happy. Try to hold the thought for as long as possible. It is ok if you can't focus for long, and your mind starts to wander, keep practicing, and your ability to focus will improve.

As your emotional control improves, try to hold more and more mundane or emotionally neutral thoughts in your mind. Emotionally weak lines of thinking can be regarding your profession, education, or really anything that does not trigger emotion in you. More emotionally neutral something is, harder it will be to focus on it while being distracted by the feeling triggering songs.

Step 4: At the end of each session, remember a positive memory to return yourself to a positive mental state. This is a significant step and should not be skipped. This step is to make your overall perception of the exercise more positive. It will help you keep yourself motivated for continuing emotional training.

Do this exercise twice or at least once a day. Practice this, however, many times as it takes for it to become easy for you to center yourself and keep yourself emotionally neutral while listening to music. How many times you will need to practice this depends entirely on your genetics and life experiences but do not be discouraged. In the end, as with everything else, practice makes perfect, and as long as you follow the steps, your emotional control will improve over time.

Exercise 2: Train yourself to deal with the aggravation

Now we will move from music to more direct negative stimulus

Step 1: Watch news reports, read articles, or watch political speeches that trigger aggravating emotions in you. Emotions can be frustration, anger, irritation, etc. Progressively increase the level of emotional aggravation as you become more proficient at controlling your emotions. Each session should last no more than 10 minutes just like in the previous exercise. Split each round of training into two parts and expose yourself to at least 2 aggravating stimuli during each session.

Step 2, 3, and 4: same as in Exercise 1.

Exercise 3: Train yourself to deal with bad memories

As the title of Exercise 3 says, now we move from external stimuli that induce negative emotions to internal stimulus, specifically bad memories.

Step 1: Recall bad memories in such a way that it triggers associated emotion. Start with memories than are only slightly negative and work your way up, just as in previous exercises. Memories like your boss yelling at you, getting a low score on an exam, a fight with your partner, etc. are all examples of bad memories.

Only use one bad memory per session. All other things practice just as you did during previous phases.

Step 2, 3, and 4: same as in Exercise 1.

Exercise 4: Train yourself to keep calm during a whole emotional movie

Watch a horror movie or some other equally emotionally charged movie once a week and try to remain calm and composed all throughout the film. Use whatever technique you deem necessary to achieve the goal.

Exercise 5: Train yourself to be calm and composed during a rollercoaster

Now, this is a bit extreme and is not something everyone will be able to master. As the title suggests, get on a rollercoaster designed with the explicit purpose of inducing fear and excitement. Try to remain perfectly calm as the rollercoaster does its things, use any technique listed previously for the purpose. If you can keep calm and composed while being spun, thrown around, flipped upside down, etc., then you indeed are a master of your emotions.

Congratulations, *if you can complete all 5 Exercises, you will be able to face up to most of life's challenges with poise.*

How to deal with Emotional Blows through contextualizing

In life, many a time, whether we like it or not, bad things happen. Negative occurrences can then color a person's view of the world and can adversely impact their entire life. For example, if your boss is an obnoxious individual who makes you jump through hoops day in and day out, it can get wear thin very quickly. A question that often gets framed is "I am a good person, why is this happening to me." Many people then derive from this question the answer, if being ethical, kind, and helpful does not get me anything, then why not be unethical and selfish. Needless to say, when enough people start looking at the world this way, everybody in society ends up suffering. It is essential to look at the bad things that happen to you, as well as the people behaving negatively, in a constructive way.

Seeing things in positive manner is critical if you wish to avoid becoming bitter, resentful, or even hateful. Research has shown that living life of anger, bitterness, and hatred is not just bad for you psychologically but is also harmful to your physical health. Also, if you are bitter and angry all the time, other people will avoid you and that too is a recipe for a disastrous life. In short, having a positive frame of mind is quite literally critical to all aspects of your life.

So how do you build a positive frame of mind, when surrounded by so much negativity? One way to deal with negativity is to contextualize reality. That is you have to look at reality in such a way that the negativity and positivity make sense.

The way I make peace with the world is by conceptualizing the Universe as deterministic, and maybe this will work for you too. In this conception, everything that happens is simply a step in the natural progression of the Universe from one state of existence to another. This is to say, I believe that every event that occurs is an equally inevitable consequence of the creation of the Universe. Whether it is something small like you stubbing your toe or something massive like a star going supernova, it is all equally important and inevitable. All events are simply the result of the Universe moving from one energy state to another. This means that every choice we think we are making today was in fact made at the moment of creation of the Universe or Cosmos. Whether it be the discovery of penicillin, which is saved 100s of millions of lives, or the various massacres that killed millions, they were all equally inevitable. From the perspective of life forms stuck at a single point in time (causal chain), it is natural to ask why did this happen, but that doesn't it was chance.

There is an easy way to understand this, consider the behavior of children. If you have a child or a nephew, niece, or can recollect your own childhood, you might remember that back then everything seemed larger than life. Every event was a life or death situation, every pimple, every low score on a test, was the end of the world. I am 35 now, I don't know if it is old enough to have this thought, but to me today those worries are childish. Looking back at my own teenage years and the years I spent depressed, I often wonder why I was so upset. Back then, it made me so unhappy that my then girlfriend did not like me as much as I wanted her to.

Today, I cannot for the life of me remember why this dearth in affection mattered. I spent 7 years wanting to die. Of course, it was the result of long-term depression, chemical imbalance, medical condition, etc. I know the science behind it, but that is not the point. Why did I care so much? It makes me laugh when I look back at the events of those 7 years. Reality is that for most human beings, it works this way, we look back after a few years and go, why did we think that was so significant.

This is especially funny to me these days. When I spend time with my nephew, sometimes he will want to play some game, and I will say no.

He is usually a good sport about it, but sometimes he will start crying. It is like by refusing to play with him, I have rejected him and hurt him deeply. A small child's memory being what it is, he cannot conceptualize time. It doesn't matter if I tell him we can play in 20 mins. It doesn't matter to him that we played just a few hours earlier. Every time he behaves this way, I am reminded of my bout with depression, and the reality of how most people see the world. Sure, people understand time, we know every rejection, and every bad experience is not the end of the world. We know life is full of ups and downs, but while the threshold may be higher, is the average human being really all that different from my nephew? I don't think so. Job loss, relationship break downs, business failures are enormous events in an individual's life, no doubt, right? But are they really?

Our current scientific theories tell us that our Universe could be many more billions of years old than we previously thought. That the Universe has gone through multiple big bangs, from birth to death, to rebirth, in what could possibly be an endless cycle. So then, why you? Why did that bad thing happen to you? Why that? Well, the honest and most straightforward answer is that there were fluctuations in the primordial energy matrix and then that bam lousy thing happened to you.

To put it another way, the Universe was born and lousy things happen. A little more drawn-out reply is that nothing happened to you, you are what is happening, what has happened and what will happen.

You are the result of an infinite number of events that came before you, and everything you do will add to the endless amount of events that will come after you. For example, if a few incidents in your boss' life were different, he may have been a very different person, and wouldn't have fired you. The causal chain is thus an eternal story; to quote Shakespeare "*All the world's a stage, and all the men and women merely players.*"

To put in another way, asking why something happened to you is just as meaningless as asking why you feel thirsty. You experience thirst because without water you will die. If you are born, then you will experience the uncomfortable sensation that tells you to drink water.

Similarly, if you are born, everything that must happen for you to complete your journey will happen. Why? Because your path isn't just yours, it belongs to the Universe. Each and every person is part of the story of the Universe and plays a critical role in making the story unfold.

Everything is always as it should be. For me, if I did not go through 7 years of depression, I would not be writing this book today. I do not see myself as being separate from the Universe. The duality of you and the Universe that we perceive is an illusion.

The duality is a trick of our senses, a perceptual error, and a limitation inherent to our level of consciousness. The perceptual error is ever-present and permeates every aspect of our being. Physical reality itself is an illusion. What we think of as physical, is an approximation of the interaction between electromagnetic fields that are characteristic of matter. The purpose of this approximation is to allow us to undertake tasks that will help us meet our evolutionary need to survive and reproduce.

Two ancient Hindu principles speak to the concept of the unity of the individual and the Universe. The ideas are "Aham Brahmasmi" and "Tat tvam Asi." "Aham Brahmasmi" means you are Brahman or you are God. "Tat tvam asi" translates to "It is you," the "it" in the phrase refers to Brahman. However, do not confuse the Hindu Brahman for the Abrahamic God, they are very different. Brahman is impersonal, hears no prayers, and has no characteristics, whether physical or emotional.

Brahman refers to the primordial energy that manifests as everything in the Universe. According to Hinduism, everything in the Universe is Brahman, including you.

Hinduism says that the ultimate goal for every Hindu's life should be to achieve a conscious union with Brahman. To unite with Brahman, Hinduism says you must see past the illusion of you as a separate entity and realize that you and the Universe are one and the goal of every Hindu's life should, therefore, be to see the Universe and Life as they actually exist, instead of the illusion that we think of as reality. This is what is referred to as attaining "Moksha" or Enlightenment. You do not have to concern yourself with Hindu philosophy unless you want to; I simply wanted you to know what inspired me to look at the world this way.

As I have stated earlier, I am an agnostic but within the Hindu tradition. While I have not achieved enlightenment, and I doubt I ever will, I do try to look at the world this way because it has many benefits. For example, because I do not see myself as being separate from the Universe, and I also do not see myself as distinct from other people. I, therefore, value all life to the same degree I value my life.

One way to conceptualize this would be as if the Universe was a human body and all people are atoms within that body. Each atom plays a role within the human body. Now, some tasks may be more glamorous than others like eyes over genitals.

Some functions may seem more important than others, like brains over kidneys, but ultimately, they are all critical to human existence. Each person or event is a part of the causal chain, a part of the story of the Universe, as it walks one more cycle of creation and destruction.

None of this means you are not responsible for your actions or that you are absolved from your duties. The Universe is eternal, and as a part of that Universe, so are you. But as every organ must do its part for your body to function, so must each life form do its duty for the Universe to make its journey. The struggle to walk your path is what gives meaning to your life.

To use a metaphor, just as a chair is not a chair if no one ever sits on it, you are not you if you do not do your duty. It is the struggle to walk your chosen path that gives life meaning. The metaphysical angst your unconscious Emotional-self experiences is the Universe's way of telling you to get off your butt and shoulder your responsibilities. What is your duty?

Generally speaking, the purpose of life is to survive and reproduce. Beyond that, it is your job to determine the path your life must take. It is a choice which you will need to make, based on an honest judgment of your innate talents and shortcomings.

Now every human wants to be happy. In fact, the saddest part of the human condition is that everything we do, we do in an attempt to achieve happiness and yet things go so horribly wrong so very often. As hard as it may be to accept, from the biggest massacres to the most courageous sacrifices, all human actions have been attempts by people to find contentment. Whether it is someone risking their lives to save a child or someone killing a child, most of the base cognitive processes involved are the same. People act in ways that they feel are in their best interest. For some, it might seem like sacrificing their lives to protect their family is the thing to do. For someone else, it might seem like killing their own child is what needs to be done. The difference usually lies in biology, upbringing, and environment. Some people are more aggressive, and some docile, some are manipulative and cunning, and some clueless, that is life. However, at the core, the differences between people are far fewer than we would like to believe.

So in the end, one, everything happens because it must happen, so forgive and do not judge. Two, the Universe needs you to try to be the best you that you can be. Three, walk your path the best you can but do not be attached to the outcomes for that is beyond you. Four, it is for the Universe to decide what must be, and what should be, will be.

If you see the world around you using these 4 principles, you will always be at peace because everything, both positive and negative is simply a part of your journey.

How to Negotiate with your Emotional-Self

As we have discussed many times throughout this book, every human being has at the very least two centers of will. The first and most potent center of willpower is your unconscious or instinctive Emotional-self or System 1. The second source of will is your conscious Logical-self or System 2. Modern theories on decision-making tell us that there is a constant battle for dominance going on in your mind between your instinctive Emotional-self and Logical-self. The struggle is over which part of you gets to make the decisions and which desires you act out in the real world.

Roughly speaking 95% of the time, people make decisions based on their instincts rather than their rational thought.

Some examples of choices we make based on intuition are who to trust, who to spend time with, what to eat, what profession to follow, what car to buy, what house to buy, etc. You unconscious Emotional-self makes these decisions based on the general principle, if this worked for your evolutionary ancestors, it would probably work for you.

The unconscious Emotional-self contains an extensive list of dos and don'ts that deeply affect our lives, even though we are barely aware of it. For example, a person's scent is used by the unconscious to decide if they carry crucial genes that strengthen the immune system. If your brain decides that they have the right genes, you will like the person's scent and are then more likely to like the person.

Of course, this does not mean every piece of advice your unconscious Emotional-self gives you is in your best interest. Your Emotional-self's playbook is quite literally millions of years old, and therefore, it makes mistakes when advising you about what to like and what not to like. An example of this mistaken priority we discussed in the first chapter, concerning how our Emotional-self makes us crave high-calorie foods.

Your instinctual desires affect almost every decision you make, yet few people exert any conscious control over this part of their psyche.

Even when people exercise conscious control over their Emotional-self usually they do it by suppressing their emotions, which is never a good idea. Suppressing your feelings only leads to internal conflicts, unhappiness, anger, frustration, etc. Nobody can achieve meaning and fulfillment if they are at war with themselves.

What is suppressing your emotions? **When you ignore what your emotions are telling you, or worse, you admonish yourself for feeling a certain way that is suppressing of emotions.** When you do this, you are conveying to your Emotional-self that you don't care about its judgments. Think about it like this, if someone you are close to told you that they don't care what you think, then what would your reaction be? Not well, right? Your Emotional-self will react to your admonishments the same way you would, after all, it is you. *Quite simply, if you don't listen to your Emotional-self, it will make your life hell.*

However, your Emotional-self is not really a rational decision-maker so you can't follow its advice either but fear not, there is a solution. The solution to emotion problem is negotiating with your Emotional-self instead of suppressing it. How do you bargain with your Emotional-self?

Simple, the same way you make peace with any other person. If you want someone to listen to you or do what you say, then you give them something in return. You can also threaten to take something from them if they don't listen to you. This is known as the carrot and stick approach.

For example, the government wants you to pay your taxes and to encourage your government says pay your taxes or we will send you to jail. Occasionally governments will announce tax amnesties or rebates to get people who may not have paid their taxes to pay. This is the essence of the carrot and stick approach. It is "give and take," the cornerstone of human civilization.

The carrot and stick strategy then leads us to two questions. What does your Emotional-self want, and what is it afraid of losing? ***In simple terms, your emotional-self wants emotional stimulation.*** Your emotional-self wants to experience emotions, mostly positive but occasionally a few negative emotions as well. Ultimately you, as in the conscious logical-self, are in control of your body. Therefore you and only you have the power to give your Emotional-self what it wants or take it away if you so chose. Actions that generate desired emotions usually correlate with behaviors that were beneficial to our evolutionary ancestors, such as eating high-calorie foods.

The following are some of the ways you can build a productive "give and take" based relationship with your Emotional-self.

- *The most natural reward to offer is a good meal.* Most people appreciate a good meal. A good meal makes most people happy or at least happier. So, if you wish to get your Emotional-self to go along with a less emotionally satisfying decision, then offer to buy yourself a good meal if it cooperates. For example, you have to study for an exam, and your Emotional-self wants to go out. You can compromise offer to go out to your favorite restaurant if you Emotional-self relents and helps you study.

- *Other rewards can be sexual stimulation, listening to music, movies, a night out, etc.*

These are some standard carrots you can use in the carrot and stick approach. In more technical terms, these are Positive Reinforcements in Operant Conditioning approach to negotiating with your Emotional-self. The stick or the Positive Punishments options are as follows,

- You could threaten to force yourself to watch a boring movie, one you hate

- Another option is watching a boring TV show

- You could visualize in your mind the negative emotional consequences of your Emotional-self not following your lead. A couple of examples of adverse results are your parents or spouse being disappointed in you, or your peers looking down on you.

In the Positive Reinforcement technique, it is things that made you happy that you offered to your Emotional-self. In the Positive Punishment method, it is things that make you unhappy that your emotional-self is being warned about.

Then there is also Negative Reinforcement approach, where something your Emotional-self enjoys is taken away as a punishment if it does not cooperate. For example,

- Not being able to play games

- Not listening to music

- Not going out for a month

Overall a combination of negative and positive approach is the way to go.

Do not keep offering the same enticement because there is a point of diminishing returns. For example, if you go and eat out every day or week, then it will mean less to you than if you did it once every 3 weeks.

To succeed, you must clearly visualize in your mind the reward or punishment, so that your unconscious Emotional-self understands what is at stake. *Verbal arguments will have less impact than visual ones. Your "arguments" will only work if what you are imagining triggers an emotion. Emotional-self can be motivated only by emotional arguments not by logical-arguments.*

For example, if you are offering to reward yourself with an ice-cream, then picture it clearly in your head till you feel like going out and eating now. If you are threatening to punish yourself by watching a terrible movie, then mentally visualize it such that it triggers dread and a desire not to do it. The key here is to convey to your Emotional-self in the language it understands that cooperating with your decisions will bring substantial benefits in the future. The unconscious Emotional-self only understands the language of emotions, so feelings are the way we must communicate.

Additionally, there are two things you should keep in mind.

First, if you promise a reward, then follow through because if you flake on promises the trust between you and your Emotional-self will decrease. The trust between your Emotional-self and your Logical-self is central to your long-term wellbeing. Second, do not use punishment methods too often. Punishments that are too strong will sour the relationship between you and your Emotional-self, and you really don't want your Emotional-self hating you.

How to reshape your identity or core behavioral predispositions

Identity is a set of ideas and relationships through which you define yourself. Many a time you find that people are more attached to their identity than they are to even their physical bodies. People are often willing to kill or even die to protect the ideas and relationships they define themselves by.

This drive of people to define themselves through ideas has massively impacted the direction of human history. Whether it is fighting over religion, nationality, ideology, or some other affiliation, the drive to protect our metaphysical-self has played an enormous role in making it happen. While most wars are a result of economic interests rather than identity-based, the financial resources gained through war are often controlled and enjoyed by the few.

The leaders start wars for economic reasons, but the people who actually do the fighting and the masses that support the wars, do so based on identity and not economics. You can force people to fight through threats, but a motivated and disciplined force is necessary if you wish to win a war. How then do you get a soldier or the people of a nation to put in that extra effort that can be critical to winning a conflict? Well, you tell them that their identity is under threat.

The irony is that most of our metaphysical-self is created between the ages of 5 and 10. More often than not as adults, we have no clear idea as to what many of the ideas that make up our identity are. This usually happens because as we grow up, we may adopt values that contradict our childhood values. Our conscious-self may realize that some ideas are immoral or lack value in the eyes of others, and thus, we may reject them. Also, if your relationship with your parents is not favorable, you may reject the ideas they taught you. However, that doesn't mean that your emotional-self has rejected those values. If these ideas were important to you when you were a child, then odds are they are still a part of your core identity.

An example of behavioral issues arising out childhood identity is the Inferiority Complex.

This issue is generated as a result of a child's need to construct a positive identity at a time when they had little to be proud of. How much a child succeeds in creating a positive identity depends on what small individual accomplishment he or she might have and the group identities they have at their disposal. Children who fail to construct a favorable identity develop an Inferiority Complex. There can be many reasons why a child might fail to build a stable sense of self. For instance, children who don't get much attention from their parents can feel unwanted and may develop an Inferiority Complex. An inferiority complex can then lead to a plethora of problems in later life, such as low confidence, lack of ability to take criticism, risk-averseness, etc.

Conversely, Children who succeed at this to a high degree may develop a superiority complex. A child who has a superiority complex might fail to live up to expectations. This mismatch then triggers a life long struggle to defend their sense of superiority from any dissonant information. This creates a dual personality of superiority and inferiority complexes. People who have a superiority complex can be combative, rude, can lack compassion, etc.
Superiority and Inferiority complexes are, however, just one example of how some aspects of your identity may be harming you.

Our personality and behavior as adults are greatly affected by our childhood sense of self and relationship with our parents. The techniques listed below are meant to help you to recognize parts of your childhood identity that may be harming you and help you change it.

Mind you, this won't be easy, of all the things written in this book, changing your sense of self is probably the hardest to accomplish. We can break this into three different parts.

- Finding out which ideas and relationships are central to your identity

- Figuring out why something is essential to your sense of self

- De-emphasizing the harmful aspects of your self-image and strengthening the beneficial parts of it

Finding out which ideas and relationships are central to your identity

The best way to answer this question is to ask yourself, what makes me happy, angry, annoyed, or aggravated. The more extreme your emotional reaction is to something being said, the more central to your identity the topic of that conversation is likely to be. In a step by step format, it is as follows.

Step 1: Write down what makes you angry and make a list.

You can enlist the help of your friends, parents, spouse, or other individuals who are close to you and know you well. Ask them if they remember a particular instance where someone, including them, said something and you became angry, irritated or defensive very quickly. Some of the things that other people say may be uncomfortable to you but do not reject it out of hand. If you feel what someone is saying maybe untrue, then corroborate by asking other friends or relatives, no matter how uncomfortable it might be.

Step 2: Analyze the incidents in the list to figure out what made you angry

Try to figure out why you got angry, irritated, or defensive on each occasion. You can use the self-awareness technique to try and figure this out. However, analyzing incidents to figure out what exactly upset you is not an easy thing. If you rely only on your own opinion, you can more likely get things wrong than right.

There are a thousand different reasons a person could get upset, and it can be difficult to isolate one reason. Let me give you an example, say someone insulted your mother with a particularly nasty swear word right to your face.

Most people, when abused in this way, become angry, but some don't. Most individuals would reply to a swear word with an equally acerbic retort. Many might skip that step and proceed directly to violence. A fair few will walk away, and a small number of people will respond with a more measured reply. Let us say you are someone who swears back with an equally acerbic response.

What does your getting angry when some insults your mother and insulting them right back in the same vein tell us about your identity? The most straightforward answer is you are close to your parents. It means you define yourself as the son or daughter of your parents and that the relationship is central to your sense of self. Does everybody close to their parents respond angrily when a parent is insulted? Not necessarily, a lot of the time people who react strongly are people who are not close to their parents but want to be. To such people, letting slide an insult to their parents would be like letting the world know that they are not close to their parents. Therefore the person reacts strongly to an insult to convince both he and others that he loves his parents.

This is not to say that every person who insults back is doing so to cover up a sense of guilt or shame at not having a close relationship with their parents.

Many, if not most people, insult back because that is what is expected of them. People don't want to lose face in front of others and be considered a coward who won't even defend the honor of their parents. Such behavior on itself says something; it tells us that the person cares about the opinion of others. How strongly someone reacts to such provocation may correspond to how afraid they are of losing face and how much they care about external validation. Someone who cares a great deal about the opinions of others will undoubtedly be unsure of their identity. They are uncertain of who they are as a person and hence rely on other people to shore up their sense of self. Such people are often described as having low self-esteem or an inferiority complex.

As we can see from this example, a particular incident and how someone reacts to it can say a lot of things about the person. In fact, it can mean so many different things, that relying on just one opinion to figure out what an incident means is not a good idea. You should ask for help from your friends and family members. You could even consult a professional psychotherapist if you are so inclined. Mind you, don't take the word of other people at face value, including those of the professional psychologists. You should ask multiple people's opinion about the same incident to get a well-rounded perspective.

Do not contradict people when they are giving their views, just listen to them. Analyze what they said at a later time to prevent any cognitive dissonance from dissuading you from confronting the truth.

Keep in mind, if you ask for opinions of other people, you may receive some outright rude or even ugly feedback, so be prepared for that. Do not let negative feedback get you down. Ultimately one person's opinion is just that person's opinion nothing more. Do not take anyone's advice at face value, and always analyze things from multiple perspectives. I know I am repeating myself, but a lot of people are very vulnerable to negative feedback. Unfortunately, many people get a perverted thrill out of saying negative things about others, so be careful when soliciting opinions.

If you are a sensitive individual, who is vulnerable to negative feedback, then be extra careful about whom you rely on. Only once you have opinions from multiple people should you use self-awareness technique to work out, which all perspectives are right. Keep in mind, none of the answers given by other people may be right. All this might sound like extra work, but your goal here is to better yourself and lead a meaningful and fulfilling life. A little extra one-time effort in return for a higher chance at long term happiness is not such a bad deal, is it?

Once you have figured what things define you as a person or what things are most important to you, then you can move on to the next step. Try to get as complete a picture as you can of what defines you before moving on. The things that define you will invariably be connected to each other, so having a complete picture of who you are will make the next step much more doable.

Step 3: Figure out why you care about the things you care about
Why you like or dislike something mainly depends on two factors a) genetic predispositions b) memories and associated thoughts. Figuring out which recollection or predisposition is the origin point of which aspect of your identity is very difficult. Also, it would be hard for anyone to assist you in this as the number of people who know you well enough to help will be minimal, if not none.

One possible avenue for help is consulting a Psychotherapist. However, consulting a professional can be costly, and the unfortunate reality of the profession of psychotherapy is that it is less of a science and more of an art. The opinions and effectiveness of therapists can vary significantly as the therapist themselves can have biases that influence their judgment.

In my personal experience, finding a Psychotherapist who can help you is almost as hard finding a life partner. I am not saying this to dissuade you from seeking help but merely so that you have appropriate expectations when consulting a professional. In the end, it is you who should do the heavy lifting. If you rely on other people to tell you who you are, or why you like something, then you are more likely to get wrong answers than right ones. However, a professional therapist is still your best bet for help when it comes to identifying your weaknesses and strengths.

A rule of thumb you can usually follow is that closer something is to your heart, more emotionally potent is its origin. If you care about something, but you don't know why then it is the result of either genetic preferences or childhood incidents that you can't recollect. The memories from early childhood can become disjointed and become hard to recall for a variety of reasons. The human brain continues to grow and change up to the age of 25, and so over time, it becomes hard to recollect memories from early childhood.

A way to narrow down when something started mattering to you is to track back the behaviors you recorded in step 1 to their earliest occurrence.

For instance, if the circumstances surrounding a fight or shouting match you noted in your list is similar to one from your childhood. By combining this with the self-awareness technique, you can try to figure out for how long you have cared about something. Once you figure out when you started caring about something, then you will have an easier time figuring out why it matters to you. Do keep in mind many of these preferences will go back to your childhood. Therefore, it may not be possible for you to remember what incidents led to your current likes and dislikes. Not all preferences are a result of life experiences and many, if not most, are genetic in their origin.

My own earliest memory, for instance, is one of talking to my then best friend at the age of four and trying to figure out why men and women get married. I won't go into the details of our conversation, but I figured out that it probably has something to do with why boys and girls use different toilets. Realizing that I lacked some very crucial information, my friend and I decided to set the question of why men and women get married aside. Now, this would indicate that I have always had a fascination with understanding human psychology from an early age.

My parents are not particularly into self-examination, but both my father and grandfather have an interest in spirituality and politics. Spiritual thinking, of course, is a meeting point of psychology, philosophy, and religion, this leads to me conclude that my inclination could have a genetic component. However, children do emulate their parents, so what portion of a desire is genetic is challenging to determine. Even genetic tendencies can be encouraged and discouraged through socializing. But if you suppress a child's core genetic dispositions, then it will cause internal conflicts and affect the child's long term happiness.

Step 4: Alter your behavioral predispositions

As we saw previously two factors that determine what you like is one, your genes and two, your memories. To alter what you like or dislike, you must alter how your mind perceives or reacts to these things. Likes that originate from experiences or memories can be changed, made more pronounced, or made less intense by modifying or deemphasizing memories. The methodology is the same as that discussed in the section on dealing with bad memories. Apart from deemphasizing specific memories, you can rejuvenate or emphasize certain other memories and make them more prominent.

The methodology for this is the same as described in the section on *rejuvenating your Feelings for your Spouse.* By emphasizing or rejuvenating some memories and deemphasizing others, you can alter the likes and dislikes that originate from life experiences. Desires that arise from genetic tendencies, however, cannot be eliminated or reduced in intensity as effortlessly. Suppressing genetic dispositions can result in them showing themselves in more extreme ways. Much like suppressing anger and frustration results in unexpected outbursts, stifling any genetic inclinations can create psychological pressures. The mental stress can eventually manifest itself in your behavior in extreme and often unpredictable ways.

The best way to deal with genetic inclinations is to be aware of them and improve your overall emotional control to where you can manage these desires. You can use any of other emotion control techniques listed in this chapter to accomplish the goal of controlling these impulses. An example would be the methods discussed in the section on *How to stop yourself from being attracted to someone.* If you manage the attraction impulses all the time, then your unconscious will take a hint and reduce the rate at which that desire shows itself.

That said it does depend on your relationship with your unconscious Emotional-self. If your relationship with your unconscious emotional-self is not favorable, then it will take no hints, and this will only lead to a build-up of stress. Psychological pressure will build at a slower rate if you use Emotion Substitution. The key to controlling genetic tendencies in the long-run is to reward your unconscious Emotional-self when it behaves the way you want it to behave. Cultivating a positive relationship with your Emotional-self will allow you to avoid stress. Using all these techniques, you can craft for yourself an identity based on your conscious thoughts.

Conclusion

With this technique, we come to an end up of this chapter and with that this book. We end with practical techniques through which you can modify what your emotional-self likes and dislikes. Everything we have looked at in this book is with the purpose of how you and I can live better lives as rational thinking human beings. I hope you have gotten as much from reading this book as I have from writing this book. Thank you for coming on this journey with me.

If you found this book helpful, then please consider helping other people find this book by leaving a review on the site from where you bought it. Thank you again. If you wish to know more, please come find me on thelogicalist.com.